The Tea Trolley

A Novel

REHANA ALAM

outskirts press

Outskirts Press, Inc.
http://www.outskirtspress.com

ISBN: 978-1-4787-9072-3

Cover Photo © 2017 Mairiam Quraishi. All rights reserved - used with permission.

Outskirts Press and the "OP" logo are trademarks belonging to Outskirts Press, Inc.

PRINTED IN THE UNITED STATES OF AMERICA

For my family:
Murad, Nigar, Aamer, Ali and Noor.
But most especially for Rahat, my friend,
companion and constant partisan.

CHAPTER 1

My life had been perfect till 1979 when I turned eighteen. In fact, it couldn't have been better. My childhood had been idyllic and I passed through adolescence without even a pimple on my face, to reach the threshold of adulthood. I should have been ready for what came next, but I had been lulled into complacency by the easy flow of my life.

Then one hot and humid Sunday in June as we sat at the breakfast table, my mother looked at my father and cleared her throat.

"Amna must be settled."

'Settled' was a euphemism for being married or at least affianced. My mother was married before she was eighteen, so to her I seemed to be teetering on the brink of spinsterhood.

"She doesn't have to be married right away," my mother pacified my father before he could say a word, "but it is time to find a nice young man for her."

And so began a whole new chapter of my life.

Truth to tell, my mother's plan was not radical. Many of my friends were engaged and some were even married. Without ever being actually told, I knew that I would get married around the time I graduated from college. My mother's philosophy was that girls had to acquire a B.A. degree, so that if a marriage didn't work or if it ended in widowhood, a woman could be self-supporting.

I had just completed the first year of college and I was feeling quite triumphant at not only doing well academically, but also at having had a great deal of fun. Now the long lazy summer vacation stretched in front of me and I had made plans to invest all my energies into enjoying it. But my mother's pronouncement gave me pause. Everything was serious with my mother and if she had made up her mind to settle me, she would.

My mother, Rabia, had completed two years of college when her wedding took place. She was the fourth of six sisters; and her parents, beset by so many daughters, married off the girls whenever a likely prospect asked for their hand. Rabia had imagined that she would continue her studies after marriage and so finally graduate.

But life had other plans. My father, Kamal, had just returned from UK with a postgraduate degree in Medicine. He had a junior job in a government hospital. Even though he was allowed to set up a private practice in the evenings, there was no money to do so. Rabia and Kamal could not live independently on what he earned. So Rabia became a part of a bustling family in which she was given the role of running the house.

My grandfather worked for the government but he was an honest officer. So mother's new home, while comfortable, was far from lavish. She was used to this, as her parents' home had been the same. Frugality was not a virtue but a necessity.

What my mother found amazing was that marriage had conferred an immediate mantle of age and wisdom upon her. Father left early for the hospital and returned at about tea time. During his absence mother had to see that the family was fed and watered to their satisfaction. Her father-in-law had breakfast at 8:30 a.m. A simple breakfast of toast and tea, but the tea had to be made with exactly three teaspoons of tea leaves and three cups of boiling water. Her brothers-in-law, who were close to her own age, had no specific demands. They had no fixed timings either and came and went as they pleased. But if their favorite shirt was not laundered or there were no bananas in the fruit bowl when they hankered for them, the air was rent with the cry of "*Bhabi*! I need help."

Once married, Rabia had no time for college. My paternal grandmother had a weak heart and was confined to her room. She enjoyed her ill health. She couldn't help in household chores but never failed to tell my mother how she could do them better. In this she was ably assisted by her daughter, Saima, who was younger than Kamal and the only daughter of the house. She had been married five years earlier and had a rambunctious three-year-old son. She and her lawyer husband, Nadir, lived with Nadir's family not too far away. But Saima spent most of her mornings with her mother, returning to her own home only a little before Nadir was due back from work.

Kamal had three younger brothers. Khalid, the brilliant one, was in the U.S. on a merit scholarship. The younger two were studying in Karachi. Jamal had just entered college and Walid was in high school.

It took Rabia time to learn the ways of her new home. But she didn't give up. With a doggedness that became a part of her personality she made sure that her father-in-law and her brothers-in-law always had the meals they liked, that their clothes were washed promptly and expertly, that all the requisite buttons were in place and that the snack cabinet in the kitchen was never empty. To satisfy her mother and sister-in-law took longer. She learned to grip her lips between her teeth when she was needled by them. Their requirements of her were more nebulous and their complaints far vaguer than those of the others. She could not seem to fit their vision of a daughter-in-law. If she spent time with the cook to ensure that her mother-in-law's *kichri* was made to the desired consistency, she was told off for abandoning the poor invalid.

"Young people never want to spend time with their elders," my grandmother would moan. And my Saima Phoopi would egg her on by reminding my mother of all the times she came to the house to find my grandmother lying all alone in her room. Purposely left out of the narrative was the fact that my mother had usually spent half the day in helping my grandmother through her morning routine, which Saima Phoopi seldom did, before she went to the kitchen to supervise the midday meal.

However frustrating her daily experience with her mother and sister-in-law, Rabia never told tales to her husband. She bathed and changed before his return and showed him a serene face. His work was full of frustration as it was. All that he had learned abroad seemed to be wasted in the government hospital where he was employed. Innovations, changes, improvements were opposed strenuously by everyone, from the highest officer to the lowest of the cleaning staff. He had to do the work of ten men to keep his ward up to some approximation of his own standards. He came home drained and needed a sympathetic ear, not a complaining tongue. Rabia understood this instinctively and gripped her lips harder between her teeth as she got ready for his return each day.

Kamal was a good husband. Silently, but unmistakably, he made it evident how much he needed and relied on Rabia. 'I love you' was not a sentiment which was vocalized in my parents' time. But Rabia could translate correctly the smile in his eyes whenever he saw her and the reverence in his touch. Her return for this gift of love was to make his home a peaceful sanctuary for him. In pursuit of this she persevered to keep all family members happy even though she continued to fail in one quarter. She knew when her mother-in-law lodged complaints against her by the emergence of a deep furrow between Kamal's brows. It was to his credit that he never taxed her with them. And his silence strengthened Rabia's resolve to win over her mother-in-law's heart somehow.

About two years later, when my mother was expecting my older brother, her first child, a terrible tragedy struck the family. Nadir was killed in a traffic accident, leaving Saima a widow. After the initial shock it was Rabia who gave voice to what was in every one's mind.

"Saima and her boy should come and live with us now," Rabia said, and everyone looked at her gratefully. My grandmother finally saw Rabia's worth for she, more than anyone else, knew that Rabia had no cause to like Saima.

Saima did not move in with them, for her in-laws did not want to lose the daily presence of their grandson. She opted to cement her recognized position of an elder *bhabi* with her in-laws rather than becoming an object of pity in her parents' house. She still came over often enough to visit her mother, but now Rabia was never made the butt of the duo's criticism. Life had dealt too harsh a blow for them not to have mellowed. Besides, neither one ever forgot Rabia's spontaneous offer of a home to Saima and her son.

My brother, Nadeem, was born and life for my mother became even easier. She had by now grasped the art of running the house, of pleasing all its denizens, and on top of that she had given a grandson to the family. Her star was in ascendance. But my mother remained as dogged as ever. She had decided early on that the joint family system was not for her. She wanted a home of her own and saved every penny toward it.

When Nadeem was two years old my father was offered the use of a doctor's office for a few hours every evening at almost nominal rates. Kamal started his private practice in the rented space, and at first the office remained empty of patients. He started wondering whether even the small sum he paid as rent was worth it. It was Rabia who supported him during this period. She shored up his confidence in himself and kept the fires of hope burning. Finally, the few referrals from his friends started to multiply. Satisfied patients were his best advertisement and his practice began to flourish. This spurred Rabia into action. She began to scour the classified section of the newspaper looking for flats for rent.

One day when Kamal returned from work, his favorite meal awaited him. Rabia had taken special care in getting dressed that day and was looking resplendent in pink. Nadeem had been put to bed and the rest of the family had already eaten.

"I have found a reasonably priced two-bedroom flat to rent," she said.

"For whom?" asked Kamal, looking up from his plate.

"Us."

"Us?"

"Don't you think we should have our own home now? Nadeem is two and we should be thinking of another little one soon. We can't keep living in one room. Soon Khalid will be back and he will be getting married. We can't all fit in this house."

My father was flabbergasted. He had given thought to nothing beyond his work. The mechanics of his home had never needed his attention. Rabia had oiled the wheels so well. But now her few succinct sentences made sense. Yet...

"We can't afford to rent a flat and an office, my practice isn't bringing in that much."

"I have savings," said Rabia. "You don't have to worry." And so they moved out of the family home just a week before Khalid's return, bequeathing their room to him.

I was born in the flat, our first nuclear family home, where my mother opted to work like a demon. She did everything herself: the cleaning, the cooking, the laundry and, of course, caring for us. She saved and saved. She made it possible for my father to concentrate on his career and become a famous doctor. Finally, Rabia had enough in the bank to have a house built which would reflect my father's position. When we moved into our new abode she hired a full complement of servants and transformed herself into a lady of leisure.

I have only a vague memory of the flat. The house on Link Avenue was my real home. It was not very large with just three bedrooms, but it was elegant and comfortable at the same time. Once my mother moved in she decided to study interior design, horticulture, flower arrangement and the culinary arts. With her peculiar focus, she mastered them all. Her house became a showcase for all the skills she had acquired. Our garden, no bigger than a postage stamp, so to say, won horticulture prizes in its size category. Each room in our home was furnished within a tight budget but followed a theme and a color scheme that made it perfect and comfortable. My mother's dinner parties became famous for the delicious cuisine and the decoration of her dining table. She invited friends and relatives, of course, but also people who would help my father's career and those who could be of use in Nadeem's future life. She made being a wife and a mother her life's work and left little to chance. She had no time to squander. She was a woman driven to succeed.

So when my mother said that she intended to get me settled, I knew my goose would soon be cooked. Yet there was nothing that I could do. My friends were going through more or less the same scenarios uncomplainingly and would consider my objections silly. Nadeem Bhai was in London working toward Chartered Accountancy. I had no one to whom I could unburden my soul except poor Zahid Bhai. Remember Saima Phoopi's rambunctious three-year-old? Well, he had grown up to be a serious young man, a doctor and a special pet of my father's.

Zahid Bhai had changed during the years he had been living as a fatherless addendum to his grandfather's family. His father, Nadir, had been one of six siblings. Nadir's two older sisters were already married and living in other cities at the time of his death. The three younger brothers were close to completing their respective degrees. Soon after Nadir passed away, one by one, the three began their careers, got married and started their families. In that burgeoning household, Zahid Bhai became more and more sidelined and Saima Phoopi's position became increasingly amorphous as the wives of the three younger brothers found their feet. The income for the family was being brought in by the three surviving brothers, the grandfather's pension being negligible. Saima Phoopi and Zahid Bhai continued to be made welcome in the family but they had to accept their inferior position. Notwithstanding his grandparents' love, Zahid Bhai knew the house in which he lived was not really his home.

We knew of the tribulations faced by Zahid Bhai as an orphan who had had to keep his feelings fiercely in check for years. When his cousins received gifts of toys and baubles that his own mother could not afford, he did not even take up offers to play with them. His devotion to his studies became his armor and he retreated to the room he shared with his mother, using homework as an excuse. His uncles and aunts did not include him in family outings, and sometimes even forgot his presence in the room when good-ies were being distributed. He hugged his pride to his chest and declined the offer of the delicacy from the hands of some younger cousin, even if the proffered item was his favorite.

He learned to let his hurt scab over and made sure never to touch the wound himself. Ignoring his pain became the norm for him. Another person might have become bitter or, at the least, recal-citrant, playing out his discontent at home and raising hell outside. But the once bratty child became silent and thoughtful. He could see no way out of his situation. There was not enough money to set up an establishment for himself and his mother. He did not expect that living with his mother's family instead of his father's would bring any material change in his life. And it would cause bad blood with his paternal uncles who would view such a move as a slap in the face of their generosity. Besides, he did not want to abandon his grandpar-ents, who loved him dearly. So he set out to convince his mother and grandparents that he was content with his lot, that there was nothing amiss. In the process he became gentle and kind and forbearing, a superb student and an all-time favorite of my father.

Zahid Bhai secured admission at the most prestigious medical college with ease and by the time I entered college he was a full-fledged doctor. Unfortunately, his income was still too meager for him to move out of the ancestral home. But he was actively pursu-ing the idea of going abroad for further qualifications. Once he had that under his belt, his salary would be ample enough to set up an establishment for Saima Phoopi and himself.

My father always had a soft spot for Zahid Bhai because he was the son of his only sister. Moreover, his orphan status wrung my fa-ther's heart. But when Zahid Bhai opted for medicine as his career of choice, my father had been completely won over. My scholarly efforts and Nadeem Bhai's were compared to our detriment against Zahid Bhai's achievements. It was only because of Zahid Bhai's sweetness of temper that we didn't end up hating him.

So now that I was faced with the threat of being settled, I turned to him. When Zahid Bhai and Saima Phoopi came to visit next, which was the same week as my mother's declaration, I indicated to him that I needed his help. Leaving the three older people in front of the TV, we walked out into the garden.

"There are going to be mosquitoes here," he warned. But mosquitoes were the least of my problems.

"They are planning to get me settled, Zahid Bhai," I blurted out. "At least Ammi is."

"What do you mean?" He looked puzzled.

"You know, find me a bridegroom."

"Hmmm," he said.

"So what should I do?"

Zahid Bhai remained silent for a while and then said, "You must do what your parents want you to do. It is not unreasonable on their part to see you married. And I am sure they will wait till you graduate."

"Yes," I said, "but I don't want to get engaged right now."

"Why not?" he asked. "It is the first step toward marriage and everyone gets married after all."

"You haven't!" I pointed out.

After another pause he looked at me and said. "And where would I take my bride? To the small room allotted to us by my uncles, and where would I get the money to care for her? You know I cannot marry till after I have a foreign postgraduate degree."

"And when you do, will you get married?"

"Yes, I suppose so."

"But, well, I don't want to get settled just yet," I repeated.

"Okay, then what do you want to do?"

I was stumped. I had no great ambitions. I just wanted to be unattached and carefree and not become responsible and boring.

I was still debating whether to be candid with Zahid Bhai, when he said," I think Kamal Mamun, your father, would agree to a postponement of this settling down business if you really had a plan to replace it. Do you have a viable alternative?"

"No," I said frankly. "But I will give it thought. Will you help me?"

"Of course. But how?"

"It will just help me to know you are on my side."

"Always," he said. And we walked back to the TV lounge.

After Zahid Bhai and Saima Phoopi left I fell into a deep reverie. It wasn't that I didn't want to get married at all. Of course marriage would be good. For one thing I would be able to do all that my mother had put under the heading of 'you can do that only after you are married.' Make up, going shopping with friends, getting a really short hair style, even singing romantic songs, fell under this category. And the list was growing longer and longer as I grew older. So I knew I had to get married and get a taste of life. But must I be tied to someone even before I left my teen years? Moreover, he would be young too and consequently poor and we would have to live with his family. Did I want to contend, at this stage, with a host of demanding in-laws? No and no again.

So I needed to have a plan that seemed right to my mother. The older sister of a friend of mine was still single at age twenty-three. But she was in medical college. Laila, a neighbor who was in dental college, was also unattached. But I didn't like either profession. I was truly stuck.

The next morning, finding that my mother was humming as she ironed her clothes in preparation for a ladies' lunch, I approached her.

"I'll do the ironing, Ammi you sit down."

She stopped humming and said, "What do you want? I don't think you can iron this. The fabric is a bit delicate."

"Well," I said, hesitating, "I need to talk to you."

"So talk," she said and began humming again but more softly.

"Ammi, must you get me settled just now? Can't we wait till I graduate?"

"Of course we will wait till you graduate," she said. "I just want you engaged now and even that will take a year most likely. It is a long process and not entirely in our hands."

"But can't we wait to begin the process after my graduation?"

"Then you will be twenty-one (she was good at math) and the window of opportunity will be nearly closed."

"What window of opportunity?"

My mother switched off the iron and sighed. She sat down and pulled a stool close to her, inviting me to sit.

"*Beta*," she said, "one has to be practical in this world. Being a spinster is not an option for you. Do you see how poor Saima Phoopi has no home of her own and she lives on sufferance with her in-laws. It would be more or less the same even if she were to move in with us or your father's other brothers. A woman is queen only in her husband's house. So you have to marry."

"I know that, Ammi," I began, but she put up her hand.

"Let me finish," she said. "So now that we agree that you have to marry, your father and I would like you to marry the best possible person. He won't be perfect but then neither are you." She didn't soften that with a smile. "However he must come from a family more or less like our own and he must be educated and earn well. Now such young men are few in number and they can have the pick of the available girls. You are from a good family and your father is well known and well thought of but you are a bit on the short side and, though pleasing in appearance, you are not beautiful."

That put me in my place.

After a pause Ammi said, "But at the age of eighteen you are at your peak. Most girls only go downhill in their appearance after this. Besides, young men who are looking to get married range from twenty-five to twenty-nine years of age and they look for girls who are between eighteen and twenty-three. That is your window of opportunity. But with each passing year there are fewer men in the right age group, for they get married, and your own bloom becomes staler. The longer you wait, the less likely you are to marry a young man with the most desirable qualities. Now do you understand?"

I understood. I was also a bit disillusioned. There did not seem to be any romance in this marriage business, only calculation. My mother seemed to read my mind.

"I can't be fanciful in choosing a husband for you," she said. "It is too important a task for me to allow emotions to lead the way. We have to be practical and plan things out. I want to see you happily settled."

"Ammi, but what about love? Shouldn't there be love in a marriage?"

"Of course, there will be love. When you get married to the right person from the right background there is no reason why you will not love each other. *Beta*, you know in our culture love comes after marriage." I was about to raise another point but Ammi had had enough of me. Leaving me with my mouth at half cock she resumed her ironing.

I retired, chastened. My days of freedom were over. The hunt had begun in earnest.

CHAPTER 2

The very next day my mother informed me that Azra Khala had a likely aspirant to my hand. The young man was twenty-seven years of age and had just returned from the UK with an MRCP. Doctors had great cachet in our house and so my mother had asked Azra Khala to arrange a meeting.

I was not quite as hopeful as my mother about the eligibility of this doctor. Not because I knew anything about him but because of a lifetime of knowing Azra Khala.

Azra Khala was the fifth girl in the family and only eleven months younger than my mother. But she got married a good five years after Ammi. The reason was obvious. Unlike her older sisters, Azra Khala was plain of face and dark in complexion. For years after my parents were married Azra received no marriage proposals at all. Because of this inordinate delay in getting hooked she managed to graduate from college. In the meantime, people would often come to my grandparents' house in search of a likely daughter-in-law, expecting the same fair skin and delicate features that the four older girls had made famous. Then they saw Azra Khala and left never to return. It must have been pretty soul-destroying for Azra Khala, more so when even the youngest sister was married before her.

Anyway, she finally got an offer of marriage when she was twenty-two years old. My grandmother felt this was Azra Khala's last chance and wanted to accept the proposal. But Azra Khala did not agree, and for good reason. The man in question was about fifteen years her senior, a widower with a 10-year-old son. He worked at a bank but seemed to have reached his career peak. He was also rather stout and bald and lived in the wrong part of town. But my grandmother persisted in presenting his good qualities. Finally Azra Khala hit upon a compromise. My father had always been her favorite brother-in-law. She told her mother that if Kamal Bhai approved of the gentleman she would marry him. My grandmother consented at once. The very next day, without having bothered to consult my father, she assured Azra Khala that Kamal approved of the proposal and within six weeks Azra Khala was married to Najeeb Khalu.

As can be inferred, it was not a happy union. It must be admitted that Azra Khala tried hard to make peace with her new circumstance. But Najeeb Khalu turned out to be a thoroughly boring individual. His only activity was going to the office. For the rest he had no friends, no hobbies, no interests and no desire to do or learn anything new. When Azra Khala complained to her mother she was given a tongue lashing.

"Does he womanize?" her mother wanted to know. "Does he beat you? Does he waste money outside the house? Then what are you grousing about, girl? Be grateful and take care of him."

Azra Khala felt alone and abandoned. My mother had her hands full with her own problems and so Azra Khala resolved to take charge of her life. No, she didn't divorce Najeeb Khalu but she made him redundant.

The biggest thorn in her side, apart from the dull and ambitionless husband, was his older sister who lived with them. Baji, who had never married, had been running the house for her brother since his first wife died. And now she hated the advent of Azra Khala. At first Azra Khala had no idea why she could not make friends with Baji. It was companionable to have another female in the house and Azra Khala had imagined them doing household chores together in amicable harmony. She had envisioned chatty mid-morning coffee breaks, going shopping together and sharing confidences. But she was frozen out of Baji's life right from the start and all she encountered from that quarter were baleful glances and cold sighs.

It took Azra Khala some time to figure out the reason for Baji's antipathy. But once she did, all her problems were solved.

About six months into the marriage Azra Khala had won over

both her husband and her step-son. Only Baji was holding out. One day as Azra Khala was clearing things away in the kitchen after dinner she happened to look up and catch Baji staring at her. The look in Baji's eyes stirred a chord in her memory. With a bit of effort she remembered where she had seen the same look before. It was years ago in Class Five when her painting had been chosen to be exhibited with those of the senior school students. Nina, who had been acknowledged the best artist of the lower school till that time, had given her the same look. As if she were a usurper. Oho, Azra Khala thought, Baji is yearning for her old place of importance in the family. In typical Azra Khala fashion, she handed it to her on a platter.

Azra Khala cajoled Najeeb Khalu into permitting her to look for a job and within a few weeks she got a position with a multinational paint company. In those days educated females from good families rarely worked outside the home. So Azra Khala was snapped up in no time. Once she started working she handed over the running of the house to Baji. All became right with the world. Baji was happy to get her old job back. Najeeb Khalu and his son continued to be well looked after and Azra Khala escaped the tedium and monotony of her married life. Moreover, the household income increased appreciably.

Azra Khala worked through two pregnancies and returned to the office each time within eight weeks of the delivery. Baji was ecstatic as her responsibilities increased and Azra Khala managed to climb up and up the corporate ladder. By the time her children were in elementary school Azra Khala had resigned from the company and opened her own interior design business. All the contacts and know-how that she had gained at her job now came into play and her business boomed. In no time she was able to buy a house close to ours and move in. Najeeb Khalu still went to work but only out of habit. His financial contribution to the family became miniscule yet Azra Khala always gave him the respect due to the head of the household and praised Baji for being the best sister-in-law in the world.

Outside the home, however, Azra Khala had a reputation of being a foul-mouthed business woman who reveled in being bitchy in her dealings. She never hesitated to crush her competition or to erupt in raucous laughter at their defeat. If remonstrated for her killer instinct and sharp spirit of competition, she pointed out that she was not playing games but running a business and winning was the only acceptable outcome.

⸻ ⦿ ⸻

On the appointed day Azra Khala came over after lunch. She wanted to check what I was going to don for the important occasion and what eats Ammi was preparing for the guests. She was wearing one of her signature outfits: a multi-colored *shalwar qameez* and a zany striped *dupatta* in shocking pink and butter yellow. From the time she started her own business, Azra Khala also began cultivating a strident persona. She was not pretty so she decided to be different. Her voice became louder, her vocabulary decidedly brazen and her clothes positively garish. She wore hues that not even the most fair skinned among us would risk, let alone someone who was as dark as she. But all this got her noticed. Rich housewives with no style of their own admired her for her eccentricities.

Azra Khala approved of the menu but my entire wardrobe was consigned to the devil.

"Haven't you got some bright, eye-catching clothes?" she asked in her stentorian voice. "Who the hell wants to see a girl in dead colors? Do you want to be rejected by your very first marriage prospect, girl?"

"I wouldn't mind," I murmured.

"What?" She raised her voice higher. "What the hell are you muttering; don't you want to get married?"

So I told her that no, I really didn't at this time and that I was just going through the motions to please my mother. Azra Khala looked at me long and hard and then sat down on my bed.

"Tell me all," she ordered. So I related my talk with Ammi and my own desire to continue my happy-go-lucky college life for a few more years and maybe even have a career. Azra Khala listened intently and then gave me a hug.

"You have a really smart cookie for a mother, you know," she said, "and you must do what she wants you to. Take it from me, it is shit to be left on the shelf when all your friends are getting married."

Then she took off her shoes and scooted up to the headboard where she placed my pillow at her back and made herself comfortable. "Sit by me, you moron, and I will tell you a story."

THE STORY OF THE ELIGIBLE ORPHAN

The deal was clinched when, through the slightly ajar kitchen door, he saw her throw a *chappati* expertly on the griddle. He became certain he wanted her for his bride.

They both worked in a semi-government organization but in different departments. Since there were only a handful of female employees in the entire office, he had known of her and surreptitiously checked her out over the past two years. The office gossip was that she was abnormal and utterly frigid since she responded with warmth to nothing and no one. She was tall, lissome, fair and extremely attractive. She did her work with efficiency and was unfailingly polite to all. But she did not have a romantic bone in her body because not a single seeker of her good graces had ever elicited even a smile from her.

During the two-year period Dilawar had become more and more aware of Raeesa. For one thing Raeesa was too attractive to be overlooked and, secondly, Dilawar was won over by her virtuous bearing. He was a Pathan and ambivalent about women working with men at all. But if their circumstances obliged them to work outside the house he would want them to be aloof and untouchable like Raeesa.

He did not pursue his interest like any other interested male would have done. He continued to monitor Raeesa's movements but did nothing overtly till he was sure that she was really as pure as she looked. Then he told his mother about Raeesa. His mother immediately wanted to know whether she was a Pathan. Dilawar's mother was not one to approve of new-fangled ways such as men choosing their own brides. The age old custom was that you married a girl picked by your family, which ensured that she was a cousin or at least came from good Pathan stock.

Dilawar should have done the same a good many years earlier. He was in his 30s, but then he had always been different. He did his duty toward his mother and sisters and took his role as the head of the family very seriously after his father's death, but he was not one to bow to traditions as a matter of course. No woman had caught his fancy before Raeesa, certainly none that his mother suggested. Now when he approached his mother about Raeesa he did not brook any opposition but silently gave her a telephone number and told her to call and set up a meeting.

Dilawar's mother complained bitterly to her daughters, both of them happily married to Pathans, about her son's non-traditional ways but she could do nothing but acquiesce. Dilawar's sisters sided with their mother on this issue but, like her, were powerless. The call to Raeesa's family was made and a date set for the meeting.

It was on that fateful day as Dilawar, his mother and both the sisters entered the drawing room of Raeesa's house that he witnessed her *chappati*-making prowess through the door which was slightly open. Somebody, perhaps Raeesa, quickly closed the door when the voices of the guests were heard. But the verdict was in! A woman who was easy on the eyes, who could work in an office setting without her name getting besmirched in any way and who could also cook was a prize indeed.

When Dilawar and his female entourage returned home he told his mother of his resolve to marry Raeesa. Dilawar's mother was quite impressed by Raeesa's looks and even liked her parents but she was neither a Pathan nor a cousin. However, after a bit of drama Dilawar's mother agreed to the match. Her daughters were more vocal against the idea of a non-Pathan *bhabi*, one, moreover, who was so old. They were certain she was not a day younger than thirty and probably even older than their brother. Dilawar silenced them by pointing out that Raeesa's age was his problem, not theirs, and a marriage proposal was formally sent to Raeesa's parents.

Contrary to Dilawar's expectations, he did not receive a prompt or positive answer from Raeesa's parents. After ten days of waiting he made his mother call them. The answer floored him. They were considering the proposal and would let him know the answer in due course, but definitely within the year.

And why was Raeesa still unmarried at the ripe age of thirty-one? This was Karachi in the early 1960s. Pretty, educated girls from good families were snapped up before they were twenty. Yet Raeesa was single.

The story began many years earlier. Raeesa just had one sibling, an older sister, Maryam. She was spectacularly good-looking and so was married at the age of eighteen to Aziz, a young man who belonged to a famous family and was just a final exam away from completing his Law degree.

The match may have been envied by many a mother of mar-riageable daughters but the union did not work. Maryam was gen-tle and sensitive and the house she went to was dominated by a stern father-in-law and an unmarried sister-in-law who were both tyrannically autocratic. Her husband proved to be incapable of any emotional attachment to his bride and so left her to fend for herself.

The father-in-law and the much older and embittered sister-in-law informed Maryam that her ways had to change since noth-ing she did was up to their standards. Her desires were ridiculed and her wishes thwarted. She was not allowed to visit her parents' home on her own and when the parents came to see her, the drag-on of a sister-in-law never left her alone with them.

Within two years Maryam had two children and her husband sat for and failed the final exam twice. Thereafter the father-in-law decreed that Aziz must sleep in a separate bedroom. According to the patriarch, time spent with women was not conducive to pass-ing exams.

Poor Maryam was left without even the semblance of support.

Her gentle nature continued to be trammeled in that loveless house. She internalized her misery till she was neither able to eat nor sleep sufficiently. Her body, weakened by repeated pregnancies, succumbed to the pressure and she began running a fever. Only when she was visibly ill and unable even to nurse her youngest was her ailment noticed. She was then told to pack her bags and was dumped, with the children, in her parents' house. She was instructed to return when she had recovered.

Maryam was diagnosed with TB. This was very much a dreaded disease at that time. But people did get cured with the right treatment, nutrition and rest. All this was available to Maryam but her heart and spirit were broken. She had gone to her new home ready to love and be loved. But all she found there were strict rules, rejection and selfishness. Maryam turned her face away from her babies, her parents, and her sister and coughed her way to death.

Her parents were devastated. The death of a daughter was bad enough but to lose her because of the treatment of her in-laws was unbearable. The parents were convinced she had contracted TB because of the cruelty of her in-laws. No talk of germs could assuage their sorrow. They could not forgive themselves for choosing Aziz for her. For months they wept and told the story to all who would listen. They did not even protest when Maryam's children were wrested away from their arms by Aziz's father and taken away. They wanted nothing to do with the evil household that had killed their angelic daughter.

After the floods of grief abated, Maryam's parents resolved not to marry their other daughter, Raeesa, to any man whose parents or unmarried sisters lived with him. It was decided that Raeesa could only marry an eligible orphan with married sisters. As Raeesa grew up into an attractive young woman she was showered with marriage proposals from every direction, but since none of the protagonists was an orphan all proposals were turned down.

Raeesa began to work after she completed her Masters. Sitting at home waiting for a likely orphan was not entertaining. Her demeanor in the office was a reflection of her parents' decision.

They wanted their daughter safe; not in danger of dying because of an unhappy marriage. So she showed no interest in any of the eligible, but unorphaned, bachelors at her workplace and, as time passed, she despaired of ever getting married at all.

Dilawar had been so discreet in observing Raeesa's behavior that she was unaware of his interest. When the call came from his mother to fix a meeting she was surprised. Since she knew nothing about Dilawar, she was unable to confirm his fatherless state or the matrimonial status of his sisters (if he had any). In the absence of this background information, Raeesa's parents allowed Dilawar and his family to visit, which led to the proposal of marriage and intense soul-searching in both the families.

Raeesa's parents instituted a comprehensive investigation into Dilawar's life. They found out all about his early life and education, about his prowess at inter-university sports, about his father's death and his subsequent seriousness of purpose. They discovered what real estate he owned and what his friends and his bosses thought of him.

Then the real discussions and the process of decision-making began. They did not want their daughter to get married unless her happiness was assured. But they also feared that she might turn into a dried-up, old spinster and be both unmarried and unhappy. She was close to thirty-two years of age. Would it really be better to let her remain single or should they let her chance it with in-laws? They could see that she was becoming increasingly withdrawn from the world and even from them. Her smiles had become rare. She had lost touch with her friends. They were all married and their lives had become different from hers. It was evident that even though she had the love of her parents her spirit was dying.

If Dilawar's marriage proposal had come some years earlier he would have been given a decisive 'No' without any delay. But at this juncture, and in the absence of any other eligible orphans on offer, his proposal had some weight. So after six months of spade work into his life, Raeesa's parents invited her to join the discussion. She was told that they liked what they had learned about Dilawar and that his father was dead and, thankfully, all his sisters married. But he did have a mother who would live with them. Her opinion was asked of this match.

Since Raeesa knew no young men even as casual acquaintances, apart from the men in her office whom she had always kept at bay, she held no real opinion about Dilawar. He was personable enough and he had never made any sort of advances toward her or any other female at work, which was certainly a point in his favor. But would he turn out to be a good husband? She had no idea. About Dilawar's mother, too, she knew nothing. She had looked kind and affectionate but was that only a mask worn to the house of a prospective daughter-in-law? Raeesa did what most dutiful daughters did. She left the decision to her parents.

Raeesa's parents struggled on for a few more months, alternating between hope and fear, but finally realized that no new facts were forthcoming and their decision would have to be based on what they already knew and, most importantly, on Allah's mercy. So after more than eight months Dilawar's mother got a call that the proposal was accepted.

The marriage was solemnized and Raeesa arrived in Dilawar's house as his bride.

Almost the first thing that Raeesa met with was a measure of sullenness in her husband. It was only after weeks of cajoling and good-humored pandering to his every need that Raeesa got to the root cause of his displeasure. Dilawar had felt belittled by the length of time it took for Raeesa's parents to agree to the match, especially after his defiance in choosing her against his family's wishes. He wanted to know the reason. Raeesa understood that Dilawar's ego was bruised and she decided to divulge the tale of Maryam's marriage and her parents' resolve. Her openness won him over and the initial wrinkle in the marriage was smoothed.

Then Raeesa's poor knowledge of Pushto caused problems in the household. When Dilawar's sisters came to visit or to stay for a few days, Pushto became the lingua franca in the house. That excluded Raeesa from all conversations. She felt like an alien in her own home. Finally she conveyed the problem to Dilawar since she feared that the wall of Pushto might keep her out not only of domestic dialogue, but may even bar her from liking her sisters-in-law and enjoying their company. She presented her case to Dilawar and offered to learn Pushto if he so desired.

"I would have married a Pathan if the language was that impor-tant to me," he said. What exactly was conveyed to his family Raeesa never found out, but the Pushto problem suddenly vanished.

Gradually an understanding developed between Dilawar and Raeesa. Perhaps their ages and maturity helped or their belief in each other's good will and good intentions. What left Dilawar askance was his bride's complete lack of cooking skills. All she knew was how to do *chappatis*! But she soon learned to cook in the style of his mother and he sighed with relief. His mother, who had her res-ervations about a daughter-in-law who was unfamiliar with Pathan ways, was also slowly won over by Raeesa's unfailing deference to her opinions and care for her comfort. Soon she started silencing her daughters if they dared to be critical of their sister-in-law.

It took longer for Dilawar's sisters to drop their guard against Raeesa. Raeesa was aware of Dilawar's patriarchal propensities. So she always welcomed the sisters warmly, served their favorite dish-es, insisted they prolong their stay and showered them with gifts. Over a period of two years the sisters warmed toward Raeesa and even began praising her to Dilawar and his mother.

Raeesa's hard work paid off in aces when she was delivered of a daughter after serious complications and it was made clear that she could have no other offspring. It was a real blow to both Raeesa and Dilawar. At this point Dilawar's mother and sisters came forward to console and comfort them. There was never a word of reproach for the over-age daughter-in-law who could not produce a son. Instead they wiped her tears and drew her attention to the beauty of her daughter.

Raeesa's parents rejoiced in their daughter's happiness. They realized that marriage was the result of chemistry between two people and understanding between family members. Ironically, when Raeesa's mother died of sudden cardiac failure and her father could not be left to manage on his own, Dilawar invited him to live with them. So it came to pass that a father-in-law became a part of Raeesa's household.

————))(()) ————

"You see, Amna," concluded Azra Khala, "Raeesa almost didn't get married. For years she watched from the sidelines as all her bloody friends got married and drifted out of her life. Her ego must have been in shreds. And, if she had got married at twenty she would not have had to settle for a bastard with a different ethnic background. And she may have had more than just one measly child. It was good luck and a lot of bloody hard work on her part that the marriage was successful. But you take it from me, kiddo, with every passing year the probability of a happy marriage becomes shit."

I could not see what the story had to do with me. I had no older sister, dead or alive, and my parents were not looking for an orphan son-in-law. But what did make an impact on me was Azra Khala's metamorphosis as she got into the swing of storytelling. Her voice became well-modulated and her words were not larded with curses. It was like she changed from Jekyll into Hyde right in front of me.

I finally got dressed to Azra Khala's satisfaction and even my mother nodded when she saw me. I wore a cream colored *shalwar qameez* and a chiffon *dupatta* of my mother's in swirls of three shades of pink. Of course I used no makeup. Remember that was on the list of what I could do only after marriage? But the pink of the dupatta gave my face a rosy glow and I was satisfied with my appearance.

As it happened my looks did not matter. My mother disliked the doctor on sight. He was wearing socks with sandals.

"At age twenty-seven if he doesn't even know how to dress," my mother opined, "there is no hope for him."

My father declared that the young man was 'sound' and to disapprove of him based simply on a lack of fashion sense was foolhardy. But my mother was adamant.

"If he can't get dressed properly for such an important occasion I don't think his priorities are correct," she said. "Besides, I have to base my decision on what I see and what I saw I didn't like."

She was willing to concede that his parents seemed okay but that was as far as she went. "Why should my daughter marry someone she would have to coach and train?" was her answer to my father's suggestion that I could help the doctor dress better.

This discussion took place after the doctor and family had departed and we started to devour all the sweets and savories made for them, which we had sampled only daintily in their presence. Azra Khala added her two bits and sided with Ammi.

"I think the blighter had something to hide. He should have worn dress shoes for this important interview. But if the bloody heat made him wear sandals why did he cover his feet with the damned socks? Are there warts on his goddamn toes? But you know your daughter best and so you can make the best decision," she ended meekly, as my mother winced at her choice of adjectives.

I was not asked for my view of the matter at all. It was a concession on the part of my parents to allow me to be present as they hashed over every move and word of the doctor and his parents. The fact that his mother ate the cake with a spoon and not a fork was brought up. The one hour visit of the three guests was all that the decision about my life could be based upon, so no detail was too trivial.

My mother prevailed and the doctor was scratched off the list of hopefuls. For my own sense of satisfaction I was told that the doctor's parents had called Azra Khala the next day to say that they 'liked' me. The answer given to them was code for the lack of approval from the girl's family. And so the first encounter ended.

When I next met Zahid Bhai at a dinner at Khalid Chacha's house I gave him a summarized version of the doctor's visit.

"I am glad," he said. "I have met the fellow once or twice and his opinion about himself is far higher than that of his peers. I hope he doesn't suffer a fall that usually follows such notions." Then he smiled, patted me on my head and went to refill his plate.

End of round one.

CHAPTER 3

As you can imagine, the hunt did not end there. Only a few days later one of our neighbors came over to discuss a likely candidate for my hand. Saghira Auntie was quite a bit older than my mother; actually her oldest daughter was nearer my mother's age. Saghira Auntie lived on her own, with a battalion of servants, and her one son and various daughters dropped in regularly. She was famous in our house for the long and detailed narrations of her current state of health. My brother and I had learned early to just greet her but never to ask her how she was doing. Best not give her the chance to elaborate. But Ammi was a favorite of hers since she listened to her with interest. My mother had always been a champion of doing what was right, and being a good neighbor was high on the list.

Saghira Auntie came to sing the praises of the younger brother of one of her sons-in-law. He was a barrister and having just returned from London he was looking for both a bride and a likely position in a law firm. The family was good, Saghira Auntie implied, otherwise she would not have aligned herself with them. And as for looks, we had best find out ourselves whether our appearances were acceptable to each other. My mother murmured her thanks and said that if Saghira Auntie thought the young man was good enough he probably was.

"Well, Rabia," said Saghira Auntie, "I can only tell you what I know, but what is inside someone's heart is known only to Allah. My Nammo is very happy in that family and her husband is a gem. Otherwise I would not even talk of the brother-in-law. But you know each person is different. Have them over and meet them but don't make your decision because of my recommendation. Find out as much as you can about the family and the young man. It is the question of your daughter's happiness after all."

Ammi assured her that a full inquiry would be initiated into the affairs of all the young men who showed interest in me before any decision was made. That is why she had begun the process so early.

Saghira Auntie nodded. "I know," she said, "you are sensible, you will go about it the right way." Then she sighed and continued, "In our family we have seen some terrible things. I can tell you one story which will make you shudder. It is about my ancestors, but now all are dead so I will hurt no one by relating it and you may profit by the lesson it teaches: appearances are deceptive."

THE STORY OF THE WOLF IN SHEEP'S CLOTHING

The story began more than a hundred years ago when Waheed Khanum was born in the house of Wilayat Ali Khan. In those days Afghan noblemen and chieftains often migrated to India to avoid blood feuds in their homeland or to seek their fortune. It was Waheeed Khanum's grandfather who had come to India and started to work for a minor prince in what is now Uttar Pradesh. His self-less service was rewarded by the allotment of agricultural acreage to him and his descendants. Wilayat Ali Khan, his son, found the revenue from the land to be enough to lead a comfortable life and so eschewed all work. So Waheed Khanum was born, the third child and only daughter, into the house of a gentleman of leisure.

At the age of fourteen her marriage was arranged with Bakir Ali Khan, the son of another Afghan family. Bakir Ali Khan's mother was not Afghan. She was the daughter of one of the elite of Delhi and, having been brought up more gently, had found her Afghan husband crude and overbearing. She went to her father's house for the birth of her baby and never returned to her husband. There was no divorce. The stigma would be too great. Besides, she did not want to remarry.

Thus Bakir Ali Khan was brought up in the house of an aging maternal grandfather who was quite unable to curb the young man's loose behavior and by a mother who could not deal with Afghan temperaments. By the time he was eighteen, Bakir Ali Khan frequented brothels, drank himself into a stupor most nights and was known to smoke opium when among his favorite circle of friends.

On his deathbed the grandfather instructed his daughter to find an Afghan bride for Bakir Ali Khan for only an Afghan would be able to deal with his licentious propensities. And so Waheed Khanum was brought to the house as the daughter-in-law that the grandfather had prescribed.

In fourteen years of life Waheed Khanum had never been given recognition of any kind. A female in an Afghan household was of little consequence and poor Waheed Khanum was neither pretty nor bright. As for her education, it did not exceed basic reading and writing.

Her new family was equally indifferent to her. Her mother-in-law was a timid lady who spent most of her waking hours on the prayer mat or in turning her rosary. The husband usually came home only to sleep. He had neither interest in nor fondness for Waheed Khanum. She, in her turn, had no influence over him, so, unfortunately, the scheme of Bakir Ali Khan's grandfather came to naught. How she had two daughters, one after another, was a mystery since her husband spent little time with her.

Soon after the birth of the second daughter and the death of his long suffering mother, Bakir Ali Khan caught some mysterious disease, the natural result of his dissolute life, everyone thought, and after a month of intense suffering went to meet his Maker. Waheed Khanum cried the dutiful tears a young widow was expected to shed, and continued to live as she had before.

A rude awakening came in the form of Bakir Ali Khan's long estranged father, who now wanted his legal share of the estate left by his wife and son. After that was disbursed, the young widow was left nearly destitute. There was enough to feed and clothe the mother and daughters but not enough to house them. Wilayat Ali Khan bluntly refused to look after three poverty stricken females just because they were related to him. Finally it was a relative of Bakir Ali Khan's mother who gave shelter to the waifs in his *haveli*.

Waheed Khanum's life in this third abode continued in the previous pattern. Nobody was actively unkind to her but, as a charity case, she had no position in the household. If there was a celebration in the *haveli*, a wedding or a birth, food was sent to Waheed Khanum on a big round tray by the lady of the house. On the two Eids, new clothes were made for the family of three. For the rest Waheed Khanum lived with her daughters in the room allotted to her, and her servant cooked for her family in a tiny room next door.

The years rolled by placidly, and Waheed Khanum's thoughts centered on possible matches for her daughters. She had been saving from her meager income so that the girls would not be embarrassed by too small a dowry when the time came. It was Waheed Khanum's earnest hope that her sojourn at the *haveli* would end when one of her sons-in-law would invite her to live in his house.

She was not worried about the younger, Hameed Khanum, who was turning out to be quite a beauty. But Qadri Khanum, the elder daughter, was hugely fat. She had a sweet, dimpled face, but below the neck she had become gargantuan. At fourteen she was bigger than her mother, her sister and the maid put together.

At about this time, Waheed Khanum was summoned by her benefactor and informed of a proposal for her daughter. A trusted retainer from the young man's family was to come and "see" Qadri Khanum. Elated at the prospect of a wedding, Waheed Khanum was yet worried that her poor daughter would be rejected by the *mughlani* who was coming to see her. Then the wife of her benefactor stepped in. A canny woman who had been running the *haveli* with an iron hand for decades, she was not going to be balked by the obesity of the prospective bride.

On the day of the viewing Qadri Khanum was told to wash her face and do her hair. Then she was put to bed and covered by a quilt. When the *mughlani* came for the viewing, all that was visible of Qadri was her pleasant, round face. The *mughlani* was told that Qadri Khanum had a fever and so was resting. Still, she wanted to know what the bulk was under the quilt. Waheed Khanum's maid said, as she had been instructed to do, that the younger sister had also crawled in with Qadri. The *mughlani* quite liked Qadri Khanum's innocent visage and so gave a positive report to her employers. The wedding was fixed for the following month.

It is to the credit of Mirza Sabir, Qadri Khanum's groom, that he never once taunted her about her weight and never allowed his family to make fun of her either. He was the third son of Mirza Nazir, a native of Delhi and a well-known collaborator and puppet of the English. Mirza Nazir had made a great deal of money because of his sycophancy, but when he died no graveyard was willing to give him place for burial. In the heat of Delhi's summer his body started to putrefy as his sons ran from cemetery to cemetery begging for two yards of land for his grave. Finally at *Isha* prayers the oldest son went to the *Jama Masjid* and begged forgiveness on his father's behalf. Then and only then was the funeral prayer performed and the nearly decomposed body interred.

All this had happened some years before Qadri Khanum's wedding. The sins of the father not being visited on the son, Mirza Sabir was deemed to be a suitable husband for her. He had passed the Matric exam and earned a living doing something unspecified at the City Courts. He had also bought property with money he had inherited.

Qadri Khanum was well housed and well cared for in her new role. Her husband was gentle with her and even indulgent. When after a year she presented him with a son she felt she had earned the right to ask him to give shelter to her mother and sister. Mirza Sabir readily agreed.

Waheed Khanum packed up her belongings, thanked her benefactor and his wife and moved into Mirza Sabir's house with Hameed Khanum in tow. Even as Waheed Khanum was leaving, her benefactor's wife tried to dissuade her from making the move. The old adage that in-laws and toilets are best kept at a distance was quoted. But Waheed Khanum's desire to live in a house where she had some status overruled all caution.

The fourth period of Waheed Khanum's life was a departure from the previous three. She was welcomed by Mirza Sabir and made to feel that she was conferring an honor on him by agreeing to make her home in his house. A large and airy apartment, the best in the house, was set aside for her use. A smaller room next to hers was reserved for Hameed Khanum. Nothing was done in the house without Waheed Khanum's advice and permission. All the servants deferred to her, for at a word from her they could lose their job. Qadri Khanum was happy to delegate the responsibilities of the household to her mother. Mirza Sabir also appeared to be content with an older woman at the helm of affairs.

Waheed Khanum bloomed in the salubrious air of Mirza Sabir's house. She was little more than thirty years of age but the upheavals of her life and the stringent economies she had had to practice had left their mark. Now physical comfort and mental peace combined to make her look nearly pretty. She bustled from morning till night in running the house and seeing to the comfort of Mirza Sabir and Qadri Khanum. Her heart filled with love for them both for it was because of them that she had found a place in society at last.

After a few months Waheed Khanum asked for Mirza Sabir's advice about the little property she owned. He willingly looked at the papers and came up with sound ideas for increasing the revenue. Waheed Khanum was delighted. She entrusted Mirza Sabir with looking after her affairs and felt that she had finally found the male support she had lacked in her father and husband. Her affairs prospered in Mirza Sabir's care and she had more money every quarter than ever before.

About a year later Qadri Khanum became pregnant again. This time she was unwell from the start. Waheed Khanum left nothing to chance. She took care of her daughter to the exclusion of all else. *Hariras* were made to tempt the palate of the expectant mother, fragrant flowers adorned her room to ward off nausea, rosewater massages were administered to lessen the discomforts of additional weight. It was decided to dispense with the midwife and retain the services of a real doctor. A British lady doctor by the name of Dr. Thomas began making monthly home visits. Finally the nine months passed and Qadri Khanum was delivered safely of another son. There was great rejoicing in the house. Mirza Sabir distributed traditional sweets in sterling silver plates to all and sundry.

Waheed Khanum returned triumphantly to her own room and picked up the reins of the household once again only to find that Hameed Khanum was pregnant too. How could this have happened? No males were allowed in, and Hameed Khanum never left the premises of the house. The truth was staring her in the face but Waheed Khanum chose to beat it out of poor, hapless Hameed Khanum. Mirza Sabir's third child was on the way.

While his wife was succoring his offspring with her lifeblood and Waheed Khnum was spending all her waking hours in ensuring that mother and baby remained unharmed, Mirza Sabir had time on his hands. The courts were closed for the summer. The same summer heat caused young, lithe, Hameed Khanum to wear pastel muslins which made her look like a glistening pearl. Firm, lean, untouched flesh beckoned Mirza Sabir. So he, too, found himself an occupation. What could Hameed Khanum do when her protector became her predator? There was no one to turn to and no one to ask for help. When her mother finally had time for her she wept out her plight.

Waheed Khanum was stunned. She had nowhere to go to and no one to speak for her either. Confronting Mirza Sabir could only mean disaster for both her daughters. She decided to send for the previously spurned midwife. This baby had to be terminated.

At first the midwife flatly refused. The pregnancy was too advanced to be terminated safely. Waheed Khanum just kept increasing the fee. Finally, in the dead of the very next night, in candlelight and with only her old maid at hand, Waheed Khanum assisted the midwife to do the deed. Hameed Khanum stuffed her mouth with a *dupatta* as the midwife pushed, probed and scraped inside her but by the end she had passed out. The fetus was extracted and smuggled out by the maid but Hameed Khanum began to hemorrhage. The midwife used all her remedies, tried all kinds of packing, made the swooning Hameed Khanum swallow every kind of herbal concoction and then she gave up. Waheed Khanum hovered over her nearly comatose daughter. And then suddenly the bleeding stopped spontaneously. Waheed Khanum fell down on her knees in gratitude to Allah. Her daughter was spared.

It took time for the poor girl to recover and she never again regained her pearly look. She was still convalescing when her mother found a poor relative who was enchanted to be told that Hameed Khanum's hand was being bestowed on him. When Qadri Khanum's younger son was six months old, her sister was married, with very little fanfare, to Akbar Ali Khan, a clerk in the Railway Department. He was posted in Hyderabad and Waheed Khanum was grateful that it was miles away from Delhi.

Qadri Khanum had become even fatter after her two confinements and often did not leave her bed for the whole day. There were wet nurses and *ayahs* to look after the children and her mother to manage the household. Mirza Sabir was attentive and loving toward her and always happy to fulfill her needs and whims. She loved him to the depths of her innocent heart and could not imagine a better husband.

Sometimes Waheed Khanum suggested to her daughter to do more to keep her husband's interest alive in her. But Qadri would smile and show her mother her husband's latest gift: a piece of jewelry or a silver *pandan*. There was no doubt in Qadri Khanum's mind that she was the center of his universe.

A year after the birth of the second son Qadri Khanum became pregnant again. She was even more unwell than the last time. Dr. Thomas was consulted. Qadri was prescribed bed rest and a strict diet. Waheed Khanum made it her mission in life to follow doctor's orders to the letter.

One night, after having spent the entire day with Qadri Khanum, she entered her own room with a feeling of relief. As she took off her *dupatta* she felt a presence behind her and before she could understand what was happening she found herself in Mirza Sabir's arms. She was horrified and speechless. But the caress of long forgotten male hands warmed her blood and her body responded to the touch.

Afterward she covered her face in shame and would not look at Mirza Sabir, much though he cajoled her. He left the room as stealthily as he had come. But the next night he was there again. All day long, as Waheed Khanum had given heed to her daughter's every wish, her own body had been yearning for the tender touches of the night before. When she saw Mirza Sabir in her room again Waheed Khanum felt her heart leap with both guilt and joy. By the third day she abandoned herself to the pleasures which she had never experienced with poor, departed Bakir Ali Khan and Mirza Sabir became a nightly fixture in her room.

Qadri Khanum was about six months into her pregnancy when Waheed Khanum realized she was with child. That night she told Mirza Sabir. His reaction froze her soul. He looked at her as if she had said nothing and continued to do what he had come to her room to do, and then departed in silence.

The very next evening the midwife was called again. Waheed Khanum put all the money she had in the house before her.

The midwife picked up the money. "How many more times are you going to need me?" she asked and then went to wash her hands and get ready for the procedure.

The services of the midwife were never required again. Waheed Khanum hemorrhaged as had her daughter before her, and, perhaps because she had no will to live, continued to bleed till the breath left her body. The next morning, Qadri Khanum and Mirza Sabir were awakened with the news that Waheed Khanum had died during the night of unknown causes. Poor Qadri was distraught at the loss and suffered a miscarriage. But Mirza Sabir was a pillar of strength. He took over all the arrangements of the funeral and at the same time cared for his wife in her distress. Hameed Khanum did not come even for the funeral. Hyderabad was too far and she could not travel alone. After a few months, Mirza Sabir sent a pair of gold and ruby earrings to Hameed Khanum. This was her only legacy from her mother. Mirza Sabir wrote to her that her mother's property had been sold to defray the cost of her wedding and her mother's funeral.

Qadri Khanum continued to bask in her husband's love and thanked Allah for conferring upon her such a prince of a husband. She had no more children but her two sons gave her great pleasure. She hoped they would grow up to be as good as their father.

Hameed Khanum lived a spare life on her husband's meager income. She was unable to conceive and her childless state was an abiding sorrow for her. Her husband was a mild and sweet-tempered person, happy in his life and content with his wife who made no demands on him, not even to visit her only sister.

———— ((❁)) ————

Kudos went to Saghira Auntie's power of storytelling. My mother had become so engrossed in the tale that she had forgotten to give me the 'leave the room' look. As I heard this account of perfidy, I quaked a little at the thought of marrying any man. But then I recalled that my mother was nothing if not thorough. She would look out for me. *Inshallah.*

The next day my mother came to my room and said, "Let's go through your clothes and choose what looks good on you. Then you can wear one of those outfits when someone comes to see you. As for your hair, I think pinning it away from your face suits you best."

I opened my wardrobe and stood aside. If Ammi chose something really strange I would speak up; otherwise her guess was as good as mine. Quickly she selected two *joras*, a pink one and the other turquoise. I liked them both.

"Amna, you may be on holiday from college but that does not mean that you should neglect your chores. Please make sure I don't have to see your unmade bed again," my mother said as she exited.

About a week later the barrister, accompanied by his parents and his sister-in-law, Saghira Auntie's daughter, arrived at tea time. My parents were there but so also were my oldest aunt, Lubna Khala, and her husband, Shafiq Khalu, who were visiting from Multan. My mother had expressly invited them (they were staying with Shafiq

Khalu's cousin) because she believed that help was needed in keeping all the guests entertained and, at the same time, in assessing them during their visit. She herself could not keep a hawk's eye on the proceedings since she was also the hostess and needed to be aware of what was happening in the kitchen.

Lubna Khala's shrewdness was not called into question in rejecting the barrister. He might have made me an excellent husband but he was not going to be given the chance. As soon as he and his family left and even before the leftover goodies on the tea trolley were fully consumed by us, my mother said, "What odd people! They want Amna only if the marriage can be in November."

Earlier, the barrister's mother had turned to Ammi. "My dear," she said, "we like your daughter, just as Saghira had said we would. And we like you and your family. All we want is that the wedding be held in November. That is when my daughter can come from abroad and we can't have the wedding without her. Nomi has also said that he cannot get married if his older sister is not present. So if you agree to November consider this to be a formal offer for your daughter's hand."

My mother replied," I have not made myself clear, I can see. Our daughter has just completed the first year of college. She has three more years to go. So the wedding can only be after that."

"What will a B.A do for her? My son will keep her like a queen. We want to book the ballroom of the Intercontinental Hotel for the *Valima*. The wedding has to be in November. So just say yes and we can go to the hotel tomorrow."

Lubna Khala countered with a smile, "Well, such decisions cannot be made so hastily," she said. "And this November is quite out of the question…."

"All right," said the barrister's mother, "we will let you decide. We like your daughter very much. This is a proposal for her if you can agree to the wedding in November. Please do let us know your decision soon."

I could see the barrister was a dead duck, for even my placid father was aroused. "They don't want my daughter," he spluttered after they left, "just a generic bride to sit on the stage in November. Well, they can jolly well look elsewhere for this mannequin."

I didn't even have to tell Zahid Bhai the details of the barrister's visit since all my cousins were having a laugh at my expense. I was teased as the November bride and my importance as an individual was compared negatively to things like dead ants and dandelions.

Zahid Bhai didn't laugh at me but his eyes twinkled as he said, "Well, you didn't want to get married just yet so your wish is coming true."

I hadn't wanted to get settled so early, true, but why was I attracting freak after freak?

CHAPTER 4

I called Ghazala, my closest friend, to share my recent ordeals with her. She and I had been inseparable since we were in Class Three and we were still together at college. Her father, a landlord in Sindh, had been shot dead near Thatta on the Hyderabad-Karachi road as a result of some land dispute shortly after her birth. I never really inquired into the details since, for me, Ghazala's fatherless status was the norm. Her mother, Ainee Auntie, did not remarry. There was plenty of money for a comfortable life and Ghazala was her raison d'être.

In a way Ghazala was very lucky that she had no father. It was not that I had anything against fathers. I loved mine unconditionally and he had always been my champion in his slightly absent-minded but adorable way. But since Ainee Auntie did not get married again and since she had no other chick or child, her time was at Ghazala's disposal. Ghazala had only to voice a desire for it to be fulfilled and as her best friend I, too, benefitted from her mother's indulgence.

I idolized Ainee Auntie. She was pretty and flighty and giggly and girlish but also superbly groomed and impeccably dressed. She taught us how to play cards and then played with us for hours on end. As we grew up she molded our fashion sense and even taught us how to use makeup, for after we were married. She was never too busy to take us to places to which we could not have gone on our own like the cinema or a cricket match or even for an ice cream. And she was never boring or censorious or pedantic.

Ghazala was engaged to a cousin who lived in Lahore and was at present studying at Cambridge University. She had met him a few times and quite liked him. Consequently, as my mother would say, she was settled. The wedding would take place when he returned and became gainfully employed. So she wasn't going through the torture of being presented to bizarre families like me. She listened as I poured out my grievances into her ear over the telephone.

"Let's go to Bohri Bazaar," she said in response.

"Oh! Yes, let's." She had hit upon the ideal remedy for dismal thoughts.

Bohri Bazaar was the center of the universe for us. It was a crisscross of some eight or ten pedestrian-only lanes which sold everything that a young heart could desire. Fabric, food, make-up, jewelry, even kitchen utensils and china were packed into the shops which stood shoulder to shoulder along the narrow lanes. I had nothing to buy, but a visit to Bohri Bazaar was not to be missed. I ran to get Ammi's permission, which was readily granted since Ainee Auntie would be with us.

"Wear a large *dupatta*," Ammi called out. I knew that. Bohri Bazaar was full of loitering young males who shoved, touched, even pinched, unsuspecting girls. But this negative aspect did not keep us away from the treasure troves of the bazaar. We learned to wear big, enveloping dupattas and walk in front of our chaperones to escape sneaky hands touching our behinds.

In no time the three of us were whizzing toward Bohri Bazaar. The driver stopped in front of our favorite store, under the tamarind tree. Ainee Auntie needed some fancy grocery items and we had a green *Pakola* each as the required goods were brought out for examination. After being thus fortified we entered the bazaar proper. Ainee Auntie wanted to buy some pots and pans but of course we did not go directly to that part of the bazaar. We checked out the newest fabric prints fluttering invitingly outside the shops and Ainee Auntie made some small purchases. Then we were captivated by the display of glass bangles.

"Ammi, that is the exact color of my new *jora*," Ghazala said, pointing toward a pale green and gold set of glass bangles. "Should we buy them? What do you think?"

What could Ainee Auntie think? She agreed with the apple of her eye.

"Amna *beta*, you choose something for yourself too," she urged me as Ghazala told the salesman to show her the green bangles.

"I think they are too small," Ghazala said. "Do you have a larger size?"

The salesman assured her it was the correct size and started easing the delicate glass bangles up her hand. Some lovely silver bracelets in the showcase at the other end of the shop caught my attention and Ainee Auntie came over to help me make the selection. Suddenly we heard an agonized whisper of 'Ammi' from Ghazala. We both turned and saw that the salesman was holding Ghazala's hand but instead of slipping on the bangles he was kneading it with a faraway look in his eyes. It was horrible.

In one stride Ainee Auntie was beside Ghazala. She yanked her daughter's hand out of the salesman's grip and sent the green bangles flying.

"What are you up to, you rascal?" she shouted. "Get away from my daughter, you pervert. We don't want to buy anything from you."

Then she held us both by our hands and hurried us away. What happened once our backs were turned I don't know; it would have been below our dignity to look back.

After that, we went to get the pots and pans that were needed and sat on plastic stools inside the shop, safe from prying hands, as Ainee Auntie inspected the goods. What the shopkeeper did not carry himself, he procured from other shops till Ainee Auntie got exactly what she liked. Now came the time to begin negotiations over the price. This too was a Bohri Bazaar tradition. No price quoted initially was accepted by the buyer. It was an open secret that the shopkeeper always came out ahead but the bargaining gave a sense of achievement to the customer. Anyway the transaction was finally completed, a porter was called to carry our large, rattling bags to the car and we set off behind him, ably protected by Ainee Auntie.

Instead of just dropping me at the gate of our house, Ainee Auntie and Ghazala accompanied me inside. Ghazala washed her hands thoroughly in my bathroom before we rehashed her experience with the slimy bangle salesman. I hugged her and both of us marveled at her mother's forcefulness. Soon we subsided into gales of laughter at the silly fellow's surprised look when he got the rough end of Ainee Auntie's tongue.

Suddenly I heard my mother calling my name and we both went to see why we were invited to join 'grown up' talk.

It was Ainee Auntie who enlightened us. "I am enrolling Ghazala in cooking classes," she explained. "Soon you will be running your own homes and neither one of you knows how to fry an egg!"

"Or to make tea," my mother interjected.

Ainee Auntie suggested I also join the cooking classes. Cooking held no charm for me but Ghazala's company was a big plus. I looked at Ammi who nodded.

"That will be very nice Ainee Auntie, thank you."

And so it came to pass that both Ghazala and I became the hopeful students of Mrs. Bhimjee. Mrs. Bhimjee was widely known for her culinary prowess and had published two cookbooks as well. She was the cooking teacher of choice for girls like us: Girls who came from homes where a full time male cook presided over the kitchen, effectively keeping out all the young females of the family. None of us minded this ban. Karachi was hot nine months of the year and a steaming kitchen was not an inviting place. Besides, our meals and snacks were expertly cooked and served, leaving us with no desire to change the system. Only one of my classmates actually liked cooking and forced her way into the kitchen. We loved the *chana chaat* and chocolate cakes she produced but none of us wanted to emulate her. Instead we marveled at her strange hobby.

Three times a week Ainee Auntie deposited us at Mrs. Bhimjee's house. There were four other girls in our class, two senior girls from our own college and two others whom we met for the first time. Poor Mrs. Bhimjee was very earnest in her attempts to turn us into chefs but Ghazala and I attended her classes solely to have fun.

Ghazala justified her attitude. "If Sardar doesn't earn enough to hire a cook when we are married, then he is wasting his time at Cambridge University."

We began by learning the use of the knife. None of our attempts came close to the magic of Mrs. Bhimjee's knife skills and even after three or four lessons we were holding the knife as we would a live snake. The meaning of cooking terms proved to be easier to learn, but some of the pop quizzes she administered were hilarious. One day she told us that she wanted to demonstrate how to bake a butter cake but that she had forgotten to defrost the butter. The question we had to answer was how to get the frozen butter to room temperature as fast as possible. Should we just leave the brick of butter sitting on the kitchen counter and wait or should we cut it into small pieces. What would be quicker? We were stumped.

One of the senior girls said, "Neither, let's put the butter into hot water."

That answer nearly got us into hot water. Mrs. Bhimjee was appalled at our lack of common sense and only after we had humbly apologized for our ignorance did she enlighten us that cutting the butter into small bits would help to defrost it faster. Poor Mrs. Bhimjee, all we learned from the butter fiasco was that it was rather tricky to defrost butter.

Ammi, however, did not allow me to waste my time. She quizzed me after every session about what I had learned and then once a week she and I went to the kitchen and, with substantial help from our cook, I was told to replicate a Mrs. Bhimjee dish. Most often the dish was not a success. I was told by Ammi that only practice makes perfect. However, my Bhimjee *yakhni pulao* was a success every time. I must say it did give me a sense of satisfaction.

Before our six weeks were over at the cooking school, Mrs. Bhimjee made an appointment with my mother and visited us one evening. She had an unmarried nephew for whom I seemed to her to be a likely partner. Which quality of mine appealed to her was a mystery as my success at *pulao* making had not been communicated to her. My mother asked me to be present as Mrs. Bhimjee waxed in praise of her nephew. He had graduated from college which was quite an achievement in a business family. He worked with his father in running a factory which made nails and screws. According to Mrs. Bhimjee he had a sweet temper and a friendly temperament. At this point my mother stopped Mrs. Bhimjee.

"We are looking for a professional," Ammi said. "I am sure your nephew is a wonderful young man but Amna comes from a family of highly educated people."

"Arre," said Mrs. Bhimjee, "I am telling you he has a B.A. He was the first in his family to go to college. Otherwise everyone else joins the business after high school. He is educated."

My mother demurred and again spoke of a higher qualification. "Our ideal son-in-law," Ammi said, "is a young man with a professional degree from abroad."

Mrs. Bhimjee smiled. "My nephew went to college in the U.S.A. And as for ideals, they don't always work out. Let me tell you a story of the sister of a good friend of mine." And before Ammi could forestall her, off went Mrs. Bhimjee!

THE STORY OF THE FUTILE IDEAL

She was the eldest of eight sisters and she had lived a charmed life from the moment she was born. When Nasira came into the world, her parents were young and full of hope. Next time, they were sure, it would be a son. Nasira was welcomed with open hearts not only by her parents but even her grandparents. She was their first grandchild and she was an extremely pretty baby. She had a pink shell-like complexion, black shiny eyes and a full head of black curls. She never cried except when hungry, and readily went into the arms of whoever wanted to hold her.

Her sunny disposition continued and her beauty increased as she grew older. She excelled at school and became the first female of her family to attend university. She was an outstanding student and completed her B.A in Urdu with flying colors. Right after that she married Junaid, who doted upon her. He was in the Air Force and Nasira immediately became the belle of the Air Force base.

Nasira had all the qualities to captivate the minds and imaginations of the young men who surrounded her. She was beautiful of face, looked lovely in whatever she wore, her conversation was both informed and articulate, her sentences were interspersed with romantic couplets written by masters of Urdu poetry and her house was always open for her husband's friends. The rapport between Junaid and Nasira was obvious to all and wonderful to behold. She instinctively treated her husband's colleagues as she would the younger brothers she didn't have and they responded with chaste adoration. Each one of the junior officers wanted a wife like Nasira.

In quick succession, Nasira had a son and daughter. But she neither lost her figure nor her vivacity. By some miracle the addition of the children caused no upheaval in her household and Nasira's poise and aplomb never wavered. Junaid was as besotted with his wife as ever. The children were always clean and well behaved and his home, the same bleak, grey government structure allotted to all Squadron Leaders, positively glowed with the warmth of ready hospitality.

Junaid's friends got married, one by one. But no new bride could compete with Nasira. They all had their good points but Nasira's charm and friendliness were unbeatable. However, she never lorded over the newcomers. In fact, Nasira genuinely welcomed each young wife, helped her to settle in, found domestic help for her and even shared favorite recipes. It was no wonder that they all fell under Nasira's spell.

Only one of Junaid's friends remained a bachelor. This was Khalid, a dashing pilot who had been Junaid's batchmate. Khalid and Junaid were very close and over the years Khalid and Nasira also became good friends. Khalid spent almost all his free evenings with the Junaids. The three had similar taste in movies and music. They loved convivial conversation and often chatted late into the night. Their threesome was so recognized by others that dinner invitations always included all three.

One winter evening, after the children were in bed, and the three sat listening to old Lata songs and snacking on pine nuts,

Junaid asked Khalid why he was still unmarried. Junaid knew that Khalid's mother was badgering him to tie the knot. She had given up all hope of Khalid marrying her niece. By now she was willing to welcome anyone he wanted to marry as her daughter-in-law. But even this blanket permission had not propelled Khalid toward matrimony.

Now, in response to Junaid's direct query, Khalid came clean for the first time. "I want a wife like Nasira bhabi. It is that or no marriage for me."

"You are an idiot, Khalid. Don't you know Allah broke the mold after he created my wife? There are no more Nasiras. So are you going to remain a bachelor forever?" Junaid laughed and tucked Nasira's hand in the crook of his arm.

Khalid didn't answer and soon the conversation turned to another topic. But later, as he was leaving, he turned to Nasira and said, "Bhabi, don't you have a sister for me?"

Nasira remained quiet but her mind started racing. She did not have one sister, she had seven. Three were already married and three were much younger than Khalid but Humaira, the third one after Nasira, was still single. Two sisters younger than Humaira were already married and Nasira's parents were quite worried about Humaira's prospects. As Nasira got ready for bed she considered the possibility of Khalid marrying Humaira. She knew Khalid to be eligible and she knew Humaira's marriage would be a big relief to her parents. She smiled as she settled in bed. This could be a very good idea.

In the following months the gears that Nasira set in motion started to mesh. First, her parents were informed of Khalid's potential interest and Khalid himself was told of Humaira's existence. He was urged to go and meet Humaira and her parents. He did just that a few months later, accompanied by his mother. Nasira's parents' home was all that Khalid could have imagined: simple but comfortable, overflowing with books and flowers, airy and light and with that indefinable aura of serenity.

By the time Humaira came in with the regulation tea trolley, Khalid was quite besotted with the thought that he could become related to the dwellers of this house and to Nasira. When he sneaked a peek at Humaira he could not help but be disappointed. She was fair and tall but she was neither pretty nor lively.

Later when he discussed the meeting with his mother, Khalid vacillated between happiness and disappointment. Everything was right with the family but Humaira did not attract him. Khalid's mother, who dearly wanted him to get married, told him that when girls met prospective suitors they were under strict orders to neither smile nor talk unnecessarily. Humaira probably had the qualities he wanted in a wife but she was not allowed to display them. Moreover, the family was good and exactly to Khalid's liking. Humaira was brought up by the same parents so how different could she be from her sister? His mother's arguments finally prevailed and a formal marriage proposal was sent for Humaira. It was immediately accepted.

The wedding was celebrated with dignity and style, as was the wont of Nasira's family, but without ostentation. Khalid and Humaira went off on their honeymoon and the guests dispersed. But the honeymoon was over before their stay at the mountain resort ended.

Khalid found Humaira to be stolid. Not only was she not beautiful and delicate like her sister, she was heavy and lumpy and had no waist. Her features were a coarse and thickened version of Nasira's. But worst of all she never smiled, her eyes lacked the spark of intelligence which characterized Nasira and she was devoid of both a sense of humor and wit. When Khalid said something funny Humaira looked at him with a blank expression and when he made a literary allusion she was baffled. She never had anything to say for herself. On the other hand she was ready to fall in with all his plans and suggestions. But was that dutifulness or did she really like what they did together? Khalid had no idea.

Once they were established in their home Khalid continued to nurse his disappointment so diligently that he didn't notice how well

Humaira ran the household. The house was always sparkling clean. Fresh flowers were arranged in every room. The food, bought and cooked on the tight budget of a government salary, was outstandingly tasty and well presented. They lived well within their means, since only a cleaning woman helped Humaira in the housekeeping.

When Khalid returned from work, Humaira had a cup of tea and homemade snacks waiting for him. A warm bath was also ready, even though there was no running hot water in their home, and neatly ironed clothes were laid out for him to change into after the bath. After ensuring that he was comfortably ensconced in his favorite chair with his current reading material, Humaira returned to her chores.

Khalid's mother visited a few months after their wedding. She noticed what a good job Humaira was doing of looking after her son and running the house. But when she mentioned this to Khalid he snapped back, "Yes, Ammi, but I wanted a wife not a housekeeper."

"Do you mean you are not happy with Humaira?" she asked, looking worried.

"Oh! Let it be, Ammi. Don't worry. I will deal with it," he said and left the room.

But Khalid's mother was perturbed. During the rest of her stay she tried to show Khalid that he was a lucky man to have a wife who worked so hard for his comfort. She mentioned that Humaira looked after her, Khalid's mother, very well too, and reminded Khalid that his wife never made any demands on him. Khalid listened to his mother silently.

Only once did he burst out, "These are good qualities from your point of view. I wanted a different wife."

"I know, son, you wanted a Nasira. But please don't be blind to Humaira's virtues because she is not her sister."

Khalid's mother left and life continued as before. He remained oblivious to all that poor Humaira could provide and only counted and recounted her shortcomings. After the initial gut-wrenching disappointment of not having a Nasira 2 as his wife, he became blazingly angry at his wife for being Humaira. Nothing she did pleased him. Either he kept silent or had something cutting to say to her. Their home became a field of armed truce between two mismatched people prone to bursts of unilateral attacks. Humaira spent her time in caring for her home and her husband, and Khalid either found friends with whom to spend his time or seethed with his lips clamped tight.

Humaira became pregnant, a consequence of him being young and healthy and her being available. When the baby was born and was found to favor Humaira in looks, Khalid turned away and lost interest in his healthy, bouncing daughter. Two years later a son was born and Khalid gave the baby no more thought than he had to his sister. Humaira now became even busier than before. The attitude of her husband seemed to bother her less. She was happy in her house, with her children. For the rest she let her mind conjure up a make-believe life in which her husband really loved and valued her. When Khalid actually swam within her ken, her eyes did not quite focus on him. It was best to have an imaginary husband who adored her rather than the real one who, for no reason that she could fathom, despised her.

After some years Khalid resigned from the Air Force and quickly found a job as a pilot with the national airline. The entire family moved to Karachi. Humaira was quite happy since she had relatives in the city. Besides, working for PIA meant that Khalid made more money and was away on duty for many weeks of the month.

Khalid enjoyed the long weeks of being away from home and Humaira. He spent time sightseeing, sampling different cuisines and even making friends. Slowly he felt drawn to one of the stewardesses who flew with him quite often. Saira was not Nasira, but she was not Humaira either. Khalid drifted into an affair with her which ended only when she realized he would not leave his wife. When she quit her job and got married he was actually relieved. He took care not to become too entangled with his subsequent paramours.

Humaira's life suddenly changed one day when her daughter, Asya, was about eight or nine years old. Khalid had just returned from a ten day trip. It was a Saturday and the children were home from school. As he entered the house he saw Humaira teaching little Asya how to make *chappatis* in the kitchen. Asia was giggling as she tried to handle the dough without making holes in it. Both the mother and daughter looked happy and busy. But for Khalid it was a moment of rude awakening. His neglect of the family was driving his children into the arms of their mother, the same woman whom he found to be dull and bovine. He stopped in his tracks.

"Asya!" he said sharply. "You don't have to make *chappatis*. Come here and I will tell you a story."

Asya looked at her mother in bewilderment. Her father had rarely spoken to her before. He usually relayed his wishes to his children through Humaira. Now Humaira took the dough from Asya's hands and nudged her to go to her father.

For Khalid and his family, that day became a turning point. It was as if he woke up from a trance. He started taking keen interest in his two children and their education. He had them enrolled in the best school of the city, he supervised their studies, he took them out on excursions, he set up tennis and swimming lessons for them, he even met their friends to make sure they were desirable.

The children loved the father's sudden and intense interest in their lives. Both Asya and Fareed, her brother, relished the mental stimulation of their new school and new activities. Khalid had a clear purpose in life: He would make of his children all that his wife was not. Only poor Humaira was the loser. She loved her children as much as ever but, with the typical heartlessness of childhood, they had no time for her anymore.

As the children grew older they became aware, although very slowly and reluctantly, of their father's unreasonable dislike of their mother. They also saw that he was often harsh and unjust to her and that she bore it silently. As the time drew near for the children to leave home for colleges abroad, they became closer to their mother. They began shielding her from their father's bursts of anger; they hugged her more and finally came to appreciate her silent love and her quiet devotion to their needs. After a span of barren years, Humaira's patience was rewarded and as she said goodbye to Asya at the airport, she knew that her daughter was hers again.

In fact, Asya and Fareed loved both their parents but they had learned that they had to love them separately. Theirs was not one big happy family. They belonged to two separate units, one headed by Khalid where they were encouraged to discuss serious subjects, appreciate fine arts and use their minds, and the other was under their mother where they were babied and petted and fed their favorite foods.

Humaira took up knitting and petit point with a vengeance once Fareed left home too. Khalid spent time in pointless dalliance and made frequent trips to see his children.

After getting their degrees, Asya got married to a cousin and Fareed began working. But fate had another arrow ready for this family. Khalid was diagnosed with cancer and went into a sharp decline. As he deteriorated, he dropped the last vestige of good manners as far as his wife was concerned. She was not allowed to enter his room or take care of him. He would shout at her if he saw her face, "Enough! Let me die in peace. I don't want to see you again. I have had more than enough of you all my life. Leave me alone."

Asya and Fareed looked after him and hired appropriate help as he became worse. But they were ashamed of their father, as they tried to make excuses for Humaira's banishment and Khalid's tirades.

Khalid passed away in less than two months. Humaira was inconsolable. She cried and related the imaginary tale of her happy marriage to all who would listen. From the day after the funeral she made it a point to go to the graveyard every evening with Fareed. Painstakingly she would clean the mound of earth, spread fresh rose petals on it and light incense sticks. She would then fall silent and pray. Asya and Fareed tried to dissuade her from going to the cemetery every day, but to no avail.

About three weeks later, one evening, Humaira and Fareed were walking back to the car after the ritual at the graveside when Humaira suddenly stopped and turned around. Fareed's heart sank at the thought of more of his mother's silent praying. But no, she gazed at Khalid's grave for a while, shook her head vigorously and turned to Fareed.

"This is it. I don't need to come again. Let's go home," she said and trod purposefully toward the car.

Thereafter she picked up the threads of her life and never again alluded to Khalid. If others spoke of him or attempted to condole with her, she went blank and looked at them as if they were speaking in a foreign language. She then spent time in explaining to them the intricacies of a new knitting pattern or in discussing the color combination of the petit point project she had undertaken.

———————⟨●⟩———————

Mrs. Bhimjee beamed at us in triumph. "So what do you say?" she asked. "Should I bring my cousin's family to your house?"

Ammi looked a bit stupefied. "Yes, very well," she said.

I looked at my mother in wonder. What did Humaira have to do with me? I didn't have a single sister and neither was I on the shelf. Must I now be paraded in front of some guy who made iron nails for a living?

But Allah had other plans. That very night my uncles and their families were coming over for a family dinner. Ammi mentioned that I was taking cooking classes with Mrs. Bhimjee and that she wanted to bring the family of some cousin of hers as a prospect for me. My banker uncle, Jamal, looked up and said, "Bhimjee? The Bhimjees?"

"What do you mean?" my father asked, now quite interested.

By this time the entire dining table was looking at Jamal Chacha. This promised to be more interesting than *biryani*.

"Well," said Jamal Chacha, "if President Ayub Khan was around still, the Bhimjees would be one of the richest twenty-two families in Pakistan. They are rolling in dough. They have a dozen factories here and now they have interest in the Middle East as well. Their homes are mansions and all their cars are Mercedes or Cadillacs.

They travel abroad oftener than you go to Bohri Bazaar and have homes in every big city. I heard a rumor that they were planning to buy a private plane!"

Silence reigned at the dining table. My aunts turned to look at me. I am sure they were wondering how poor little Amna could have attracted a Bhimjee. I was thinking the same. My dream of flying off to Paris in my own jet was shattered as I heard Abba say, "Well, then they are not right for us."

Why not? I felt like asking but, of course, kept quiet.

My mother nodded. "You are right, Kamal. We are ordinary people. We cannot fit in with the very rich. I will tell Mrs. Bhimjee tomorrow. I think we need more *biryani*," she said prosaically and left for the kitchen.

So I did not get to see the nail maker at all. Another bullet dodged. At this rate I could get the blithe and untroubled college years I yearned for and even set my foot on the first rung of a career! I called Ghazala and related the entire saga. She listened only half-heartedly since even her third attempt at *yakhni pulao* had failed. I told her to come over the next day and we would conquer the *pulao* together.

CHAPTER 5

The next evening Ghazala was dropped off at our house by Ainee Auntie who had to go to a funeral but she promised to return and partake of the *pulao* we were going to cook. Since my cooking expertise was being showcased for the very first time I had taken Ammi's permission to ask Zahid Bhai for dinner as well. It was going to be a party.

Ghazala and I entered the kitchen and made sure that the cook had washed the chicken and sliced the onions. I began to make the *yakhni* with frequent reference to the written recipe and asides to Ghazala. As I measured the water to be added to the chicken, the cook intervened with "*Bibi*, a little more, a little more." I told him not to interrupt because Mrs. Bhimjee's recipes had to be followed to the letter.

With the *yakhni* cooking safely under the supervision of the cook, Ghazala and I retreated to my room. We only had a month of summer vacation left to enjoy together, as Ainee Auntie and Ghazala always spent the last few weeks of the holidays in their home in the mountains. When Ainee Auntie returned we joined our mothers in the drawing room.

At a signal from Ghazala, Ainee Auntie turned to Ammi. "Why don't you send Amna with us to Doonga Gali this year?"

But Ammi lifted up her right hand in the 'halt' gesture. "Ainee, how sweet of you to invite Amna," she said, "but you know we want her to get settled. This time is very important for her, she can't be absent from Karachi at present."

Ainee Auntie nodded understandingly and asked, "So how is it going?"

Ammi elaborated, "I have told everyone that we are looking for a suitable young man for our daughter. I get phone calls all the time but many prospects have to be turned down at once since they are not our type. You have heard of Mrs. Bhimjee's nephew already. Then the other day a friend of mine called about her son. I have known her for ages and the young man is a banker but, Ainee, his father is such a miser that my friend has never had a happy day in her marriage. Knowing this I had to wriggle out of the situation somehow. It is a great responsibility to find just the right person for our Amna."

Ghazala and I had been pretending interest in our own conversation during this dialogue. But I knew Ammi had made it a point to say all this in my hearing. She was letting me know that she was being selective about whom I was presented to.

Ainee Auntie seemed to be in a pensive mood. She said, "Marriage is not all it is touted to be, you know, Rabia. One can be happy or unhappy whether married or single. I was a wife for three years and have been a widow for much longer. My husband was a fine man as *waderas* go, and never hurt or harmed me, but I can't say I regret my situation. I am now my own mistress. I do what I like and I am answerable to no one. I have my friends and my books and above all I have Ghazala."

"You are fortunate to be financially independent, Ainee. Also in that you have no son. Otherwise your in-laws may not have allowed you such a free hand with your offspring. Most women do not have your advantages. They have to live with others as old maids or widows and become unpaid drudges for their relatives."

"You are right," Ainee Auntie said with an upward look. "I thank Allah for all that He has given me. But my contention is that marriage is not a panacea or a guarantee for happiness. Let me tell you about my friend's cousin. Times were different then and women had fewer options but Abida comes to mind when marriage is being presented as the best choice for women.

A sort of desperation sets in after age thirty in females if they are still unmarried, and poor Abida was not only over thirty, she was also in a bind..."

THE STORY OF THE PARSIMONIOUS PARENT

White strands of hair glinted in her reflection. Early morning, as she performed *wuzu* for the *Fajr* prayer, was the only time she could look at herself in the small mirror over the sink. The height of the mirror was adjusted for the more important members of the house, so she stood on her toes and touched the silver in her hair.

She thought about the day before when, as she cleaned up after cooking lunch and peered in the mirror fleetingly, she got a thump on her back. "Enough preening, my princess, it is time to make the chappatis. Off you go," Mehr Apa said glaring at her. Abida fumbled at her still thick hair with trembling fingers and hurried to the kitchen.

Her hands automatically divided the dough into balls. She then expertly rolled out each ball into a perfect circle and threw it on the hot griddle. Over the years she had become so adept at *chappati*-making that her griddle was never without a *chappati*. While one *chapatti* was cooking she rolled out the next. Mehr Apa did not allow any wastage of fuel.

Abida pushed back a curl of sweaty hair with the back of her hand and wondered why she was still unmarried. Why was she condemned to unacknowledged and backbreaking toil in her father's house? Ten years ago, or to be exact fifteen years ago, women routinely commented on her smooth complexion, her classic features and thick hair. She used to laugh off the compliments then. Now the few women she met just averted their eyes. Was it her graying hair that silenced them?

She had considered dyeing her hair. Perhaps black hair would elicit a marriage proposal from some as-yet-unknown party. She felt that the only chance of escape from her abysmal condition was through marriage. But how could she dye her hair? She had no money, she was never allowed to go shopping and she had to share the bathroom with her father and Mehr Apa. The bleakness of her future brought tears to her eyes as she dropped the last chappati on the griddle.

In the seven years since Partition, she had nearly forgotten her life in Muradabad. She used to be the mistress of the large *haveli* where she was born. Cooking *chappatis* was as far from her life of ease as digging ditches. Her mother had died when she was fifteen and since then she ran the house. Hadi, her father, a man of sweet disposition, had only one obsession...spending as little money as possible. He was a miser. She had not been sent to school. According to Hadi, there was no need for her to go to school since her mother had never been to one either. But it was really a matter of expense. He did not even remarry because of the outlay of money. So Abida learned to read and write at home and was careful to remain within the housekeeping budget and thus father and daughter lived in harmony.

As Abida blossomed into a good-looking young lady, many marriage proposals were brought to the *haveli* by the local matchmaker. But all were turned down. Hadi could neither part with such a good manager for his home nor was he willing to spend money on her wedding.

"There is plenty of time. What is the hurry?" he would say, silencing the matchmaker and any relative who dared to question his views.

Time ran out when the country was partitioned and the conditions in and around the *haveli* became so fraught with danger that Hadi had to leave his ancestral home against his will. After reaching Lahore safely, he rented two rooms in the old part of town. Abida suddenly found that, from mistress, she had become a maid of all work. She had to clean, dust, cook, wash, and stitch. Having lost the income from his lands, Hadi had become more tight-fisted than ever. All he had was his wife's jewelry which he'd managed to bring with him. Every couple of months he had to sell off a piece or two and the dwindling cache of gold frightened Hadi. He had never been this vulnerable before.

Even during this lean existence, Abida's hand was sought in marriage. The son and later the nephew of Hadi's cousins sent proposals. They were declined. Hadi could not part with Abida. Who would do the work? The wedding would require a monetary outlay and some jewelry would also have to be given to Abida to avoid losing face in the family. And if he gave her the jewelry as her dowry, what would he eat? So more time passed and Abida developed calluses on her hands and worry lines on her forehead.

Then Hadi heard of the Government Claims Department. He was told he could send in a claim for the lost *haveli*. He clutched at this ray of hope. If he got money for his erstwhile home he could afford to live in a semblance of comfort. His life began to revolve around Claims offices and notary publics. He would leave in the morning and return after dark. Abida stayed at home behind closed doors and cooked whatever vegetables Hadi remembered to buy on his way home.

It was at this juncture, when Hadi was becoming increasingly frustrated with the slow wheels of the government, that he met Mehrunissa. She was the daughter of a compatriot of Hadi's. Her father had owned land adjacent to Hadi's lands and had died a few years before Partition. But during his life he had sent his daughter to school and later married her to a government servant. Mehrunissa's husband had opted for Pakistan and she had come to Lahore with him.

Unfortunately, the husband passed away shortly afterward and left her to fend for herself as best she could. She was subsisting on the charity of friends and relatives when she ran into Hadi.

It was a meeting made in heaven. Mehrunissa needed male protection and a place to live; Hadi needed a personable and educated female to further his cause at the Claims office. Mehrunissa moved in with Abida and Hadi and started to accompany Hadi every morning. In only six months Hadi's claim was approved and a large house was allotted to him in Model Town. When they moved there, Hadi and Abida were accompanied with Mehrunissa.

Mehrunissa quickly assessed that the house could be cut up into three residential sections. She found tenants for the two rental portions within months and as payment took the largest room in Hadi's portion for herself. Hadi lived in the other room and Abida slept in one corner of the verandah which was curtained off for her use.

Hadi became more confident once he realized that the jewelry could now be kept intact. There was a regular income from the rental portions. Mehrunissa made herself indispensable by taking on the job of manager. It was she who interviewed tenants when the need arose, and talked to painters and carpenters when repairs had to be made. Abida continued in the kitchen. If she had been familiar with the legend of Cinderella she would have had some hope for the future. As it was, she only developed more lines on her face.

Mehrunissa was not done yet. She was too astute not to realize that her position was precarious. If Hadi were to die she would be out on the street. She could not inherit anything as the daughter of a friend. The only way to strengthen her position in the house was to marry the owner. She knew she could maneuver the hapless Hadi into marriage and even the presence of Abida in the house would pose no obstacles to her plans. But her subsequent plans would run much more smoothly if Abida were ejected from the house. The easiest way to get rid of her was to get her married.

Now that Abida had an unlikely ally in Mehrunissa events moved very quickly. Hair dye was bought and Abida was taught how to use it. New clothes adorned her and skin lotions smoothed her hands. Abida wondered how Hadi had been persuaded to part with money for all this. In fact, he had no idea of the changes in his house. Mehrunissa had always skimmed off some of the rent and maintenance money as her due. She was spending from her own nest egg as an investment in the future.

Hadi had no desire to see anyone in the house get married. Weddings meant expenditure. Moreover, over the years his sex drive had become dormant if not dead. As for Abida, he thought she was way past the age of marriage. But he had not taken Mehrunissa's driving energy into account. He was suddenly presented with a marriage proposal for Abida and was told that Abida had already shown her acquiescence to the proposal. Before he could assemble his thoughts and put forward arguments against any imminent expenditure, Mehrunissa announced that the cost of the wedding would be borne by her as a gesture of gratefulness for all Hadi had done for her.

Hadi could see no road block in the way of Abida's marriage: He would not have to spend a *rupee* on the wedding and after Abida's departure Mehrunissa would still be there to run the house. He agreed to meet with the people who had shown interest in Abida.

They were found to be in no way suitable. The parents were crude and illiterate and clearly not from the class to which Hadi belonged. Their son was close to fifty. His face and demeanor showed he had had a hard life. He was a childless widower and worked at a menial job in Karachi. He was literate but not educated. The family, which lived in some far flung and depressed suburb of Lahore, was composed of not only the parents but a divorced sister and her brood as well. There was nothing in the proposal to recommend it. Yet between Mehrunissa's machinations and Abida's desperation it became a done deal and a date was set for the wedding over Hadi's feeble protests.

After the wedding, Abida found that she had just exchanged the venue of her drudgery. Her husband left for Karachi within the week and Abida started spending her days in the kitchen as before. Her parents-in-law, though unlettered and simple, were not unkind, but she still had to keep to a tight budget and be more or less incarcerated in the house. She was the least important adult in the house; even her sister-in-law's children treated her like a servant. If she had become pregnant conditions may have eased for her. But her age and her husband's job in a distant city were not minor obstacles.

Abida's life took an even more dire turn when she was invited to her father's nuptials to Mehrunissa. This event was celebrated with much more pomp than her own marriage. Abida realized that the doors to her father's house were now permanently closed to her. She had left her father's house out of her own volition and now there was no going back. So Abida put her head down, crushed her desires, and slaved in her new home. Once a year for two weeks, her husband came on leave. He spent very little time with her since there was so much to do for the rest of the family. She did not mind, she hardly knew him.

Time passed relentlessly. First her father-in-law and then her mother-in-law passed away. Her sister-in-law's son grew up, got a job and that whole family moved into a house of their own just as Abida's husband retired and came back to Lahore. Even then her life did not change for the better. He suffered a stroke shortly after his return and was confined to his bed. Abida looked after the house and her husband. By this time her hair was completely grey and her hands were scrubbed clean of her fingerprints.

It was a moot point whether Abida's marriage was a mistake or not. It had been her belief that marriage would allow her to escape her circumstances. But her life did not change even though she achieved her desire. In her case it was clear that in or out of marriage she was destined for adversity. Some lives are lived on a plane of suffering while good fortune is reserved for others.

I was nearly in tears. This was the saddest story I had ever heard. Poor, poor Abida!

"You can't fight your fate," my mother said, "and then she was uneducated. That is such a big handicap."

Ghazala pretended to look for white hair in my ponytail and we dissolved into giggles. With a frown Ammi told us to go and get the *pulao* ready.

We left the room and burst into laughter as we walked toward the kitchen.

"I didn't know Ainee Auntie knew such sad people," I said. "Anyway, what has Abida to do with me? My mother is alive and poor Abba is certainly not a miser."

The cook had chopped the garlic, separated the *yakhni* and the meat and even washed the rice. So we quickly completed the process and put the *pulao* on a low flame to simmer to completion. When we returned to the drawing room Abba and Zahid Bhai had arrived and the talk had turned to politics. Ugh!

Everyone loved the *pulao*. It was a hit. Ghazala felt reasonably certain that she would be able to replicate it. After a hearty meal Ghazala and I roped everyone in to play *chakri*, a sort of six-person card game like trumps. Ainee Auntie, Ghazala and I were partners and we really trounced the others. Of course we cheated. Ainee Auntie was a champ at unobtrusive cheating. That is why we had chosen her for our partner. As for Abba, Ammi and Zahid Bhai, what they didn't know wouldn't hurt them.

At 11:00 p.m. the party broke up. First Ghazala and Ainee Auntie left and then Zahid Bhai rose to take his leave. I walked with him to the gate.

"We really beat you hollow at *chakri*," I crowed.

"We would have won," he replied with a smile, "if we had cheated too."

"What! Did you know we were cheating? Why didn't you say something?"

"Of course I knew. I didn't want to expose Ainee Auntie and then you were enjoying winning so much."

Hmm. And here I thought we had fooled him.

"So how is it going with you?" Zahid Bhai asked.

"I am having a great time. The summer vacation is just flying by. Ghazala and I do something fun nearly every day."

"No, I mean what is the progress on your mother's project."

"Oh! That," I said. "Nothing much has happened. Ammi has been turning down inappropriate parties herself. So I only had to meet the doctor and the barrister. Do you know about the Bhimjees?"

"Yes, your father told me."

"Well, at this rate it may take all of three more years to settle me, so I will have got what I wanted."

Zahid stopped and glanced at me. "Is there someone you like perhaps?"

"Nope," I said, "I know no males outside the family."

"And you don't mind this process of finding a match for you?"

"There's no way out, Zahid Bhai. If I want to get married I have to submit to this process. It is not going to be easy. Ammi says I am short and not beautiful."

61

Zahid Bhai actually burst out laughing. "Yes, that sounds just like Rabia Mumani. Listen, you are not all that bad. So keep your spirits up." And he opened the gate.

"Wait," I said, "tell me how your plans are progressing."

"Nicely. I have all the paperwork done and will be soon submitting the applications."

"Then you will go? When? For how long?"

"By this time next year I should be away. I'll be gone three or four years."

"I will really, really miss you. I will have nobody to talk to."

"My mother will miss me too." He smiled a crooked smile and left.

CHAPTER 6

Even *Ramzan* did not pose any obstacles to my enjoyment of the summer vacation. In a way it was a boon since the settling business was put in abeyance for the Holy month. Ghazala and I were inseparable. I spent many nights at her house and, each time, we stayed up all the way to *sehri*, the meal before sunrise. Then after doing full justice to *parathas* and omelets we slept till *Zuhr*, the noon prayer. This way the fasting was a cinch. On especially hot days we went to the movies and between the air-conditioned coolness and the thrill of the movie itself our hunger pangs were assuaged.

Right after *Eid*, Ghazala and Ainee Auntie went away to their house in the hills. Before I could call up any of my other friends to organize some fun activities, I was told to pitch in and help with a marathon cleaning of the house. House guests were expected. Ammi's sister, Tahira, was coming from Lahore with her husband and daughter.

Tahira Khala was Ammi's number two sister, the oldest but one. Her husband, Latif Khalu, had retired as a brigadier, but he didn't quite believe in his retirement. When he asked how you were, you straightened your back and stood at attention. The points of his moustache could have shamed M. Poirot's and his voice was loud enough to carry across a football field or two. He was so proper that he even ate mangoes with a knife and fork! It was not going to be easy to have him stay with us.

Tahira Khala was even more difficult in some ways. She had been a beauty in her heyday and she thought that made her special. I became familiar with her idiosyncrasies when we stayed with her the previous year to attend her older daughter's wedding. She took hours getting ready and emerged expecting applause and compliments from all who were impatiently waiting for her. The pictures of her youth proved she had been pretty at one time but I had known her only as chunky in body and charmless in face. So the fluttering of hands and the dainty gestures that she was prone to make were incongruous, to say the least. She spent a fortune on her clothes and considered it necessary to announce the exact cost of what she had on. Sofia, her younger daughter, left you in no doubt about the price of her outfits either.

Sofia was really beautiful. She was reputed to be like Tahira Khala but I thought she was much better. People stopped in their tracks when she appeared and followed her with their eyes as long as she was visible. She was really perfect, a feast for the eyes, even mine. But her beauty was merely skin deep. She was stuck up, difficult to please and boastful. She was only a year older than I but when I was told she would be sharing my room, I shuddered. Nothing in my room would be up to her standard. My clothes would be made fun of and she would take over the entire space, relegating me to a corner. I didn't say a word to Ammi, of course, but proceeded to hide my treasures from prying eyes and to sigh in desperation.

The belief among the family was that Tahira Khala had a wonderful marriage; that she was a pampered wife and that she and Latif Khalu were highly compatible. I had my doubts. What I saw on my trip to Lahore was that they lived parallel lives. She painted and polished herself and, swathed in silks and chiffons, spent time with her bosom buddies who proceeded to massage her ego by praising her looks. Their talk centered on pricey clothes and imported shoes and cosmetics.

Latif Khalu, on the other hand, hung out with his cronies and re-hashed every battle from when he was commissioned in the army. The way he told the tale it seemed only the Pakistan Army practiced correct military strategy and the Indians were a set of cowardly rats. I know nothing about armies and fighting but to me it all sounded a tad one-sided and relentlessly boring. In the ten days that we stayed in Lahore, Tahira Khala and Latif Khalu spent no time together and didn't even smile at each other. If they were happy it was because they had learned to be happy apart. But they did use a lot of *janoos* and darlings when they addressed one another, effectively convincing even themselves that they had an exemplary marriage.

The girls, Saleha and Sofia, were the apples of the brigadier's eye. The way his face lit up when either of them appeared on the scene was quite endearing. Tahira Khala's sentiments were more reined in, but her ruling passion was to make splendid matches for them. Saleha, the plainer of the two, was married to a 'farmer,' as Tahira Khala put it. In fact he owned untold acres of fertile land in the heart of Punjab and was dripping with money. For Sofia, the beauty, Tahira Khala had decided not to settle for anything less than the son of an army general or a federal secretary.

"Why are they coming, Ammi, and why are they staying with us?"

"Why shouldn't they come and stay with us?" Ammi asked. "Tahira Apa is my sister."

"Yes, but they hardly ever come to Karachi, so what is the occasion?"

"There is a wedding they need to attend." Ammi explained. "The son of one of Latif Bhai's colleagues...."

"So why do they need to be here for two weeks? Weddings don't last so long."

"Amna, it is none of your business how long they stay. What is the matter with you? Why are you being so rude? You should know better than to question your elders. Besides, they both have lots of family here. You should be happy; you will have a ready-made companion in Sofia."

As if! But there was no more to be said and I pushed my bed to the far wall to make room for the extra bed which was being dragged in from the storeroom. What will be, will be, I thought, but there go the last couple of weeks of my holidays directly down the drain.

Eighteen-year-olds had very little say in anything that mattered. This business of agreeing to whatever was said and done by older people had never sat well with me. I kept my mouth shut, since respect for my elders had been drilled into me since childhood, but I chafed inside. Ammi and Abba were very liberal by the standards of their friends for they let me sit in on many serious discussions in the house. However, I knew by tacit agreement that I was supposed to listen but not speak.

The next day the dreaded trio arrived. Ammi picked them from the airport while I supervised one final flurry of cleaning of Nadeem Bhai's room where the parents were going to stay.

Tahira Khala entered holding her highly manicured, red-tipped hand weakly to her forehead indicating her need to rest before lunch. After a hand flutter in my direction and some muttered words she headed toward Nadeem Bhai's room. Latif Khalu asked for an immediate cup of tea and settled in front of the TV. Sofia followed me, appearing almost ethereal. All in white, a thick braid of brown hair swinging down her back, she seemed to glide rather than walk to my room.

She turned her head delicately to survey the room. "There is an attached bath, isn't there?"

"Yes," I said, "your towels are pink."

She wafted into the bathroom and the door clicked shut. I didn't know what to do. Should I wait for her in the room or go and help Ammi? At that point the driver brought in her suitcase and I had it placed on the floor near her bed. Fairly soon Sofia emerged from the bathroom. If anything she looked even prettier than before. My lips opened of their own accord and I said, "Wow! You really look nice, Sofia."

"Thank you," she said, taking the compliment as her due. "Ammi got this fabric from Islamabad. It doesn't crush. It is Rs. 200 a yard." My goodwill flew out of the window.

"Do you want to rest? Or you can unpack," I said pointing at the closet which I had painstakingly tidied so that she would have place for her things.

"Oh! You have your things in here too," Sofia said as she opened the closet door. "Well, you can ask the maid to hang up my things. But she better iron them first."

"We have no maid. But I can help," I offered.

"No maid?" Her eyes opened wide and looked truly gorgeous. "Well, in that case..."

I helped her and was told the genesis and cost of every piece of clothing.

That evening the guests had to make some visits. The three of us had a cozy dinner together. Nothing makes your own parents look more acceptable, even precious, than when you see other people's strange ones. I was asleep when Sofia returned. She switched on the light without a by your leave and opened and shut the bathroom door a dozen times. I didn't say a word; Ammi would have been proud of me.

At breakfast which was later than normal and much after Abba had left for work, I was told that some important people had been invited by Tahira Khala for tea that evening and the most elaborate arrangements had to be made for their delectation. Azra Khala was also invited.

"Oh and Zahid will also be here," my mother said. "I had asked him to come over many days ago, before I knew of your plans."

"Then it cannot be helped," Tahira Khala said. "But, Rabia, please make sure everything is of the best. I have made an appointment for Sofia's hair at Susie's and will have to go with her. So I can't help you. But *janoo* can go shopping with you and he will take his wallet with him, of course. Darling, you must pay for everything," she instructed Latif Khalu.

Ammi got up and said, "No Tahira Apa. No one needs to go shopping. You go with Sofia. All will be done to your liking."

And so Latif Khalu settled with the newspapers in the TV lounge and Ammi set off to the kitchen. Tahira Khala took close to an hour to get ready for the beauty salon, and then the mother daughter duo sallied out. I shut the door of my room with relief and curled up with a book.

Need I say that professionally done hair and makeup made Sofia breathtaking? I wished Ammi would let me get my hair done sometime. Makeup was too much to ask. Sofia walked into our room and announced that she would need the room and bathroom for two hours to get ready, meaning that I should be done with my grooming and be out of the room by 4:00 p.m. I felt like responding, "Yes, madam," but I knew it would be wasted on her.

At 4:00, with a clean, scrubbed face and dressed in freshly laundered clothes I presented myself in the kitchen. Ammi had prepared a truly sumptuous tea. I had been told to make Mrs. Bhimjee's sandwiches and so rolled up my sleeves to begin.

"Everything else is ready, *beta*," Ammi said. "Put the sandwiches on this platter and cover them with a moist towel. I am going to get ready. Also just check the drawing room in case it has become dusty again. The cook will help you if you need to get things chopped."

Abba and Zahid Bhai came home before either Sofia or Tahira Khala had emerged from their rooms. We all settled in the drawing room waiting for the guests. At exactly 6:00 p.m. Azra Khala arrived in a swirl of loud pinks and purples. There was still no sign of Tahira Khala or Sofia when five minutes later the special guests entered the room. It was a group of mother, father, daughter, son-in-law, son and aunt. They looked pretty normal to me, so why all the fuss? Abba and Latif Khalu sat by the father. Zahid Bhai knew the son-in-law, a doctor, and so he gravitated toward that couple. Ammi and Azra Khala corralled the mother and aunt and so I went to sit by the son.

He was about twenty-six or twenty-seven years old, I guessed, slim and smiley. So I smiled back and said, 'I'm Amna."

"I am Saif." He smiled more broadly. "And what do you do, Amna?"

"College," I said. "I will start my second year shortly. And what do you do?"

"I am doing Chartered Accountancy in England," he said.

"Oh, wow!" I jumped in before he could say any more. "So is my brother, Nadeem. He only went there a few months ago."

"Yes?" he said with interest. "Well, I'm nearly finished; another year and then the dreaded exams."

"Are they horridly hard?"

"Yes. Quite hellish! But I'm planning to take one of the crammer courses to improve my chances."

"Nadeem Bhai says those are for losers," I blurted out and then clapped my hand to my mouth.

Saif laughed out loud. I joined in shakily. There was a sudden silence in the room and everyone was looking at us. Zahid Bhai broke the spell by turning round to his doctor friend and continuing the conversation.

"Well, I am a bit of a loser," Saif said when the others stopped staring. "I didn't really want to do C.A. but then I didn't want to do anything else much either and one has to earn a living."

"That's just like me; I don't know what to do either so my mother is planning to marry me off." I was about to clap my hand to my mouth again but I saw Saif's eyes were dancing.

"And does that meet with your approval?"

"Not entirely," I said. It seemed I had found an ally. "I want to get married but not just yet. College is fun and I'm only eighteen."

Saif agreed wholeheartedly. "Life is fun but I am not eighteen anymore," he said, "and earning a living is soon going to become my lot. But if the world were different we could have done amazing things like go to the North Pole on a dog sled. " He chuckled.

"Or to Egypt," I said, "to discover the tomb of a pharaoh." I was getting into the swing of it.

"Or cross the Sahara on a camel. Or go lion hunting in Africa. Or climb the Everest. Or…"

"Wait, wait. Let me get a word in too." I laughed. "You can't hog up all the options." Saif's eyes were brimful with mirth. He put his finger on his lips and gestured with his other hand for me to go on.

But before I could say a word the door opened and Tahira Khala entered, followed closely by Sofia. There was a hush in the room. Sofia was looking like a princess. She was all in soft pink with fresh *motia* flowers threaded into her ear hoops. Divine! I turned to Saif but his eyes were riveted on the vision in pink. Well, no wonder.

Ammi got up and said, "Amna, I need your help." I followed her to the kitchen. Ammi gave the tea trolley a once over and then Sofia came to roll it into the drawing room. At that moment I understood. Saif was here to meet Sofia. Oh poor man. He was so nice. She would eat him alive. But there was nothing I could do. Nobody ever asked for my opinion about anything.

The tea went off well. Ammi's cooking and presentation were highly praised as always. Somebody even commented about the sandwiches favorably. Sofia sat by Saif but they were not talking much. Sofia was making no effort to make conversation and was just giving monosyllabic answers to all his questions. At one point Saif caught my eye and sighed. I smiled back. Finally the visit drew to a close and the guests departed.

Contrary to our usual practice we didn't fall on the tea things like starving locusts. We had to behave for Tahira Khala and Latif Khalu. Only Azra Khala kicked off her shoes and sat on the carpet by the trolley, the better to reach for the goodies.

"Thank you, Rabia," Tahira Khala said. "Everything was done well. You know Riaz *sahib* has just retired as a federal secretary and he is used to the very best."

"He is such a nice man," Abba said. "It was a pleasure discussing the current situation with him. He knows my friend Rizvi *sahib* very well."

Sofia remained quiet and ate nothing. Who cared? The more for me. Ammi had made her signature strawberry cheesecake and I cut two hefty wedges, one for me and one for Zahid Bhai. I knew it was his favorite.

"Here you are," I said, handing the plate to him.

"Thank you." He smiled. "How did you know I wanted some?"

"We both love Ammi's cheesecake. Since I wanted it I knew you would like it too."

We sat in companionable silence relishing the cake.

"So how is the visit going?" he asked softly.

"Rough," I replied in a whisper. "But it is two days down, twelve to go. This too shall pass."

"Atta girl." He grinned. "I expect nothing less from you. Will it help if I offer to take you girls to a movie?"

"It would help me! I love going to the movies with you and for the few hours that the movie lasts I won't need to do anything for madam."

As it happened, the program was scratched right away. Sofia did not enjoy movies. Besides, the ceremonies of the wedding they had come to attend were commencing from the next day and so she had no time. I think Zahid Bhai was unimportant in Tahira Khala's scheme of things and time spent with him amounted to time wasted. I sincerely hoped Zahid Bhai had not fallen for the pretty face from Lahore. His father was dead and had never been in the military or the government service so his chances with the beauty were zero.

"Mrs. Riaz was boring," Azra Khala said. "But the young man was damned sexy." Then turning toward me she raised her voice another decibel to ask, "Any sense in that gorgeous-looking head of his or is he the male version of a dumb blonde?"

I didn't know what to reply, or even if I should say anything. I looked at Ammi for help.

"We can look into all that once a proposal comes from the Riaz family," Ammi said in her most neutral voice.

"Of course a proposal will come," Tahira Khala said. "Did you notice the pin drop silence when my Sofia entered the room?"

Nobody had anything to say to that. Sofia, the most concerned, sat effortlessly erect and looked out the window with no expression on her face.

Azra Khala got up from the floor in a whoosh and walked toward the door. "I am doing damn-all here, I see, so I will head off home and take a bloody long nap before dinner."

"I have never understood why Azra thinks speaking in this fashion makes her interesting," Tahira Khala said with a grimace after Azra Khala left. "Who has taught her all these curses?"

"Must have been her husband, Najeeb," Abba said, his eyes twinkling. In the ensuing laughter, Sofia didn't even crack a smile and Tahira Khala mumbled something about a time and place for jokes.

Soon Zahid Bhai also departed leaving me, without a prop, to the tender mercies of Sofia and her mother. I agreed with everything Tahira Khala said over dinner and actually earned a pat on my back from Ammi as I headed to my room. As expected, Sofia was occupying the bathroom. Who knew when she would be done? I crawled into bed and, like Scarlett O'Hara, hoped for a better tomorrow.

CHAPTER 7

The next morning Sofia took out the *jora* she was going to wear to the first ceremony of the wedding they had come to attend. It was a lovely shade of yellow and had silver embroidery in an intricate pattern on the *dupatta*. I owned nothing like that. Actually I hardly had any 'wedding' type clothes. I wished Ammi would let me wear the kind of clothes Sofia wore. But no, I only had party wear made at *Eid* and *Bakra Eid* and then I had to wear the same two *joras* to all weddings and parties during the year. And even those *joras* had to be appropriate according to Ammi. They ended up looking rather juvenile and never as sophisticated as Sofia's. I recognized the fact that Sofia was far better looking than me but there was no doubt that fine feathers also helped to make the bird dazzling.

I left Sofia in the room to complete her morning regimen at her leisure and went to have breakfast. Abba had left earlier, as usual, and Tahira Khala was holding forth in a petulant voice.

"Here it is ten o'clock already and there is no call from Guddi. You know she was the one to have set up yesterday's visit. I was expecting to hear from her last night. I am sure my Sofia has bowled them over. I think I will call Guddi myself. She is a dear friend but a bit of a scatterbrain."

Both my mother and Latif Khalu looked up at this.

"No, Tahira Apa, it is still early. I don't think you need to call her, we don't want to seem too eager, do we?"

"Hmm," said Tahira Khala, "you may be right. We will wait till the evening."

For those who are uninitiated in the rituals of the arranged marriage let me explain what this conversation meant. Guddi, a friend of Tahira Khala's, had suggested Saif as a possible candidate for Sofia's hand. A meeting was set up for which my mother had to produce a delectable tea and Sofia had to look her best. Both requirements having been fulfilled, the next logical step was for Saif's mother to call Guddi forthwith and say she wanted Sofia for a daughter-in-law. Tahira Khala was irritated since this hadn't happened last night. Ammi was correct in implying that generally some days elapsed before the call came. The man's family had to be absolutely sure and weigh all pros and cons before sending a proposal; there was no turning back. But Tahira Khala also had a point since we were not talking about just anybody, but Sofia.

Ammi and Tahira Khala went out shopping after breakfast and since my room was still occupied by Sofia, I joined Latif Khalu in the lounge and wrote a long letter to Ghazala. Sofia finally finished just before lunch. I have no idea what took her so long, as she was going to the beauty parlor in the afternoon. Her departure allowed me the use of my room again and that felt good.

Abba returned about 7:00 p.m., tired but affable as usual, and everybody gathered in the lounge for a convivial cup of tea before the three guests got dressed for their evening out. Just then Tahira Khala's friend, Guddi, arrived and was greeted with great cordiality. Unlike Ammi, who always let me sit in for such conversations, Tahira Khala sent Sofia and me out of the room before a thing was said about Saif.

Not ten minutes had passed when we heard raised voices from the lounge. We could make out no words but Tahira Khala's voice was discernible and her tone suggested anger. Then Ammi came to call us back to the room. We both entered and sat in silence.

"I don't know why you needed to call the girls, Rabia." Tahira Khala was now holding forth. "You are just over-indulging your daughter. Even if the conversation is a little about her she doesn't need to be here to listen to every word."

Abba stirred in his chair but Ammi smiled at him with a shake of her head. "Yes, Tahira Apa, I know you don't agree but that is the way we have brought up Amna."

"So is there any answer that you would like me to convey to Mrs. Riaz?" Guddi asked, looking harassed.

"First," Ammi said, "just repeat what they said to you, for Amna's benefit."

Guddi looked at me and said, "They want you as their daughter-in-law. Saif has taken a liking to you."

Me? My gosh! He liked me better than Sofia? Glee, pure glee! I took a moment to remove any semblance of gloating from my expression and turned to look at Sofia. She was impassive. I suppose one person less from the long list of those dying to marry her did not really matter. Perhaps she could hide her feelings very well, or she had no feelings. I didn't know and didn't care. The warm glow which came from being preferred over Sofia was too precious to be allowed to dissipate.

"I'm not saying that there is anything wrong with Amna, but I think the young man must be blind," Tahira Khala declared.

Abba stirred again but held his peace. Ammi tried to appease her sister and said, "Everyone has his own agenda. Who knows what he was thinking?"

"Thinking? He wasn't thinking. He had come to see Sofia. He did see her so how could he reject her after that?"

"It is not a rejection," poor Guddi interjected. "It is a proposal for the other girl in the family."

Tahira Khala gave her a withering look. That turned out be the last straw for Guddi.

She cleared her throat and sat up straight. "Beauty is not everything, you know, Tahira. Girls even better looking than Sofia sometimes don't marry well. And sometimes their beauty becomes their downfall. Don't you know the story of Momi?"

Without waiting for an answer she launched into her story. Obviously, she wanted to divert our attention.

The Story of the Doomed Beauty

The first time I saw Moamer Khatoon, generally known by her pet name, Momi, was when she was pregnant with her third child. I don't remember her figure but her face was arrestingly beautiful. It looked like it had been washed with dew and dried with rose petals: soft, glowing with health and perfection. I did not know her at all, and had to ask a friend who she was. I was at a ladies' lunch in Lahore with a good twenty or more people present, but only Momi stayed in my mind.

I was informed that Momi was expecting her third child and was on her second husband. It was years later when, by chance, I was in the seat next to Momi on a long international flight that I got the rest of the story....straight from the horse's mouth as they say.

First of all, the unlikely name was explained. Momi's mother was the second wife of a businessman. She had two sons during the time that she was the favorite of her husband. As the boys grew older, and she too became more mature, her husband's eyes began to rove again. Momi's mother felt she had no way to ensure his continued interest except by presenting him with a daughter, a daughter that he did not have with his prior wife either. A baby girl was born and named Mehreen but she died before she was forty days old. A year later Momi's mother had another little girl and named her Mehreen again. This one lived all of two months. When Momi's mother delivered a third daughter she took no chances and called her Moamer Khatoon....aged lady. This time the baby lived.

Nevertheless, Momi's mother's plan did not work: She was unable to keep her husband by her side. When Momi was five years old, her father married for a third time and was rarely seen by either of his two earlier families after that. In another few years he was dead. His will came as a shock to both his second and third wives because all his assets were in the name of his sons by his first wife. The other children and wives only got paltry sums as their portions.

Suddenly Momi's mother and her children became poor. The unfortunate lady did the best she could under the circumstances. She opened a beauty salon in a room of the house in which they lived and which she had inherited from her husband. With the income she put her three children through school and college. In the case of Momi, whose looks turned out to be winsome, marriage seemed a good option, and when the neighbors asked for Momi's hand in marriage for their son, Momi's mother agreed.

This was not a decision made solely out of necessity. The young man had just returned from England with a degree in textile engineering and had started work in his father's factory. He was of the right age and personable enough. Most importantly, Momi had met him a few times, and had happily agreed to the match.

The marriage took place and, shortly afterward, Momi's siblings and mother migrated to the U.S. The first few years of her marriage went by in a daze for Momi. The very fact of not scrounging for money perennially, and having all her legitimate needs fulfilled without perpetual financial planning and manipulations was enough to keep her content.

Her husband, Azhar, was a good, moral person. He felt proud to have her on his arm when he went out. The envious gazes of other men made up for differences that had started cropping up between the couple.

But the rifts only became deeper as time went on. Two sons were born to them, but Momi had no time for either. Her success at parties, mainly due to her looks and the lasciviousness of the men around her, went to her head. She spent all her time in adorning herself and buying clothes that she had only dreamed about before her marriage. New clothes, more daring than previous ones, visits to spas and beauty salons, and the constant parties where she could showcase herself, became her life. She had no time for her sons. An appointment for her eyebrows was more important than taking them to the doctor.

Azhar gently pointed out that this was not acceptable. When she did not listen he became insistent. Quarrels became the order of the day. Azhar wanted to shield the boys from the daily domestic strife but Momi had no scruples. She would erupt in front of her sons and use foul language.

As time passed, the lives of Azhar and the boys diverged completely from Momi's. After work Azhar spent time with his sons while Momi, dressed to the hilt, attended social events in the city. During the day the children were either at school or with their *ayahs*, while Momi took care of her looks and wardrobe. After the initial spats, Azhar became silent. He hated what was happening to his family, but his innate good breeding stopped him from initiating divorce or even from continuing the futile fights with Momi in which he was usually bested by her uninhibited tongue.

Perhaps if Momi's mother had been at hand things could have taken a different course. As it was, Momi did exactly what could be expected. She fell madly in love with one of her fellow players on the party scene and, in typical Momi fashion, she did not try to be discreet.

Finally, the news of her amorous adventures reached Azhar even in his seclusion. He might still have done nothing except protect his sons from the ugly chatter about their mother, but then Azhar's parents stepped in. They did not want their family name to be tarnished and their son to be the butt of cuckold jokes. They insisted Azhar divorce Momi but she preempted him by sending him papers asking for a divorce herself.

Because of Azhar, the divorce was amicable. She did not want the boys. "He was a really good father" she confided to me, but she took all the jewelry that she had accumulated during the marriage. Azhar thought the exchange was very well worth it and held his sons to his heart as she walked away.

Azhar did not have a long life. Perhaps the years with Momi had taken their toll. He passed away while the boys were still in high school. He left instructions that if Momi wanted to meet the children in the future she should be allowed to do so. His love for his children dictated that they should not be left motherless as well as fatherless.

On the Momi front, events were more turbulent. The man she was in love with dallied with her for another year. He even provided her with a flat to live in but refused to marry her. When she finally realized that the love of her life was in fact a lowlife, her illusions were shattered. She had thought that her looks were enough to bring anyone to heel, that men would behave like Azhar when they came in contact with her. She wondered whether her looks had begun to fade. But the hot glances of the men with whom she came in contact belied that. She finally cut her losses and married the man who had been offering her the protection of his name for years. He was not her first choice but he was rich.

When I saw her at the lunch she had been married to this man, Javed, for about a year and was heavily pregnant. It was only years later that I found, in conversation with Momi on the plane, that she was not, in fact, married to the man she loved and the glow on her face was not that of happiness. It was simply habit and her role in life that she had to look radiant all the time.

She had three children with Javed. She was still not the maternal type but had to produce the children in deference to Javed's wishes. He was a bit of a dictator and did not care for Momi's whims.

When I asked Momi if Javed made her happy, she said, "He is all righ..ght." Not very encouraging, since that was also the way my neighbor categorized her relationship with her daughter-in-law. I did not probe any further, but after lunch on the plane Momi elaborated on her earlier comment. Apparently, Javed was independently wealthy, and they lived in a large house with a trained staff. She never had to do anything she didn't want to do. But Javed himself was a difficult person.

He was eccentric to the point of being nearly abnormal. Javed woke up at sunrise, had a substantial breakfast, and closeted himself in his 'office' till 5:00 p.m. During this time he needed complete silence and privacy. Momi could busy herself in any way she wanted. The children went to school, then to friends or the club and knew that at home they had to creep around like mice till the magic hour of 5:00 p.m.

At 5:00 Javed came out of his office and wanted his family around him. It was like a command performance. The children and Momi had to be home. They all then sat on the front lawn of the house and had tea and the day's news was relayed to Javed. He was very attentive and caring toward the children. He helped them with their homework when they were younger and at all times he was their confidant and fond partisan. He was the favorite parent, hands down. He knew their aspirations, their problems, their friends' names, even their secrets. Till dinner the parents and the children spent time together and then the youngsters were sent to their rooms. The 5:00 to 8:30 p.m. family time was inviolable.

Momi, the party creature, also had to be present during the family hours. Often she sat silently and dreamed her own dreams since her interest in these family gatherings was minimal.

After 8:30 Javed focused on Momi. He wanted her to be beautifully groomed and dressed so that she could dominate any party they attended as the most beautiful woman in the room. She was his showpiece. Momi was paraded as the prize that Javed had won because of his millions.

It was funny, Momi told me, now that Javed expected her to spend money on her clothes and grooming, the joy of doing so had lessened considerably. She still liked being the center of attention at parties but she did not relish being shown off as if she were a valuable possession. When she put makeup on she felt like she was an ornate silver salver, getting polished for exhibition. She knew she was being unreasonable for she had money to burn and her looks were at their peak. But she wondered why she could not get a husband more to her liking. Azhar had been boringly good and Javed was selfish and unromantic. Her looks should have ensured a perfect marriage and a perfect life.

She did not rebel against Javed, Momi told me, because she had no alternative. As she grew older she doubted that she could ensnare another rich man, so she made do with Javed. At least materially speaking, she had all that she wanted. She still turned heads when she entered a room and the lustful gazes of men still warmed her skin. And she could still spend freely on herself. Our long air journey came to an end at this point. I left Momi looking lovely but a little wistful.

Years passed and Momi was forgotten in the ups and downs of my own life. On one of my infrequent visits to Lahore I was told that Momi had lost a son to cancer. Since she was not receiving visitors I did not try to see her. But on my next visit I contacted a mutual friend and set up an appointment to visit Momi. She was a changed person. Perhaps because I was only a chance acquaintance and outside her normal circle of friends she spoke without reservations.

She told me that the fragile structure of her marriage and family came crashing down when her second son by Javed was diagnosed with cancer. Suddenly, she realized how futile her life had been. Money was not enough to save her son. She had thought that her wealth and beauty made her immune to adversity, and that trouble would never assail her as it had her poor mother. But now her son could not get well, even though money was being spent like water. He had been taken to the best doctors in the world. Even experimental drugs had been used, but he did not improve. Finally, at the age of seventeen, he died.

Momi told me that after his death she went into a deep depression. She found nothing inside her that could explain this loss or give her comfort. She mourned all those hours that she had spent on herself and at parties instead of with her son. Strangely, Javed, who had always been the more loving parent, accepted the death with resignation. He spent even more time with his surviving children. But Momi was inconsolable.

Long hours of counseling and therapy helped her to regain her composure but she came out of her ordeal a different Momi. The importance of beauty waned in her eyes. She stopped wearing her fashionable clothes and spending time at spas. The new clothes she ordered could be described as utilitarian at best. She just pulled her hair back tightly and pinned it in place, and as for her face she left it bare. Soap and water became her new best friends. She told Javed she could not waste her time at parties every night but agreed to accompany him once or twice a week if he was willing to take her in her new guise. Javed agreed. He was growing older himself and could not party as hard as before, nor did he want to spend his declining strength on keeping his trophy wife safe from predators. Besides, Momi had retained her allure even in her simplicity.

Momi started to volunteer as a helper in the cancer ward of a well known city hospital even though it drained her physically and emotionally. In an about-face, she eagerly awaited their family conclaves which were now only instituted once a week, since the children had grown up and had their own interests. She even called her children by Azhar and gradually became a small part of their lives. She told me, with wonder in her voice, that she actually liked playing with her grandchildren, something she had never imagined doing with her own.

As Momi sat next to me with her salt and pepper hair pulled back to reveal the perfect bones of her face, she still looked stunning. She told me that in her other life she might have been flying to Brazil for a face lift but that now she was about to travel to New York to be at hand when her daughter had her baby

"I am happy in a different way now," she said. "I am fifty-five years old and willing to age gracefully." She gave a faint smile and said, "My mother used to tell me that my face was going to be my destiny, but I have changed my destiny."

•《◊》•

I sighed with relief since this story, centering as it did on a renowned beauty, could not possibly be aimed at me. A quick peek at Sofia showed that she was as imperturbable as ever. Tahira Khala, on the other hand was ready to have an apoplectic fit.

"Enough of that, Guddi! For heaven's sake, of course looks matter and beautiful girls make better marriages than ugly ones. Just because Riaz *sahib's* son can't recognize beauty when he sees it doesn't mean that the rules of the game have changed."

Tahira Khala did have a point. For some reason Saif liked me better (Oh! Glory be!), but in fact I was not in the same league as Sofia.

"So what answer am I to give them?"Guddi asked again

Before Tahira Khala could start another tirade, my mother said with a placatory look, "Tell them we need time to think."

"We don't need time," Tahira Khala exploded. "We don't want anything to do with such vulgar people. Come to see one girl and propose to another one! I've never heard of such goings on."

I saw a look of understanding pass between Ammi and Guddi and then Ammi gestured to me to leave the room. I got up reluctantly and exited. Sofia overtook me and slipped into our bedroom and locked the door. I supposed she needed to get ready to go out.

That wasn't the end of the evening. Zahid Bhai dropped in after dinner to get something signed by Abba and, of course, I poured the tale of my victory into his ears at the first opportunity.

He smiled and said, "And that makes you feel good? Do you like Saif too?"

"I don't even know the guy, Zahid Bhai. But I like being preferred over Sofia the Beauty."

"Oh, you don't have to worry about that. Many men would choose you over her," he said, looking at me squarely in the eye.

For the first time Zahid Bhai's words left me bewildered.

CHAPTER 8

Tahira Khala and party brought forward their departure and left immediately after the completion of the wedding ceremonies of their friend's son. I wasn't sad to see them go. Sofia, not my favorite cousin at the best of times, had been giving me the silent treatment after the Saif fiasco, and hogging our room till I felt like an alien in my own home. Tahira Khala and Ammi remained cordial but one could feel the tension in the air when they sat together. Only Latif Khalu remained his old military self, loud and bluff.

Ghazala returned to Karachi soon after and I recounted my victory over the Beauty to her. We both felt good. Then we were catapulted into the first days of the new academic year at college. It was all exciting and exhilarating but also a bit scary.

At home the job of getting me settled went on apace. Ammi screened out the unacceptable suggestions and about once a fortnight I had to present myself, pushing the tea trolley, to interested parties. But no one came up to my parents' standards. In some cases, which I made a point of forgetting quickly, I didn't please the visitors. For the health of my ego, thankfully that didn't happen too often.

Just as Ghazala and I were settling into our new routine, Ammi told me of another imminent guest. This time Nani was coming to stay with us. I was delighted since Nani, my maternal grandmother, was a hot favorite of mine.

She had been widowed some years after my birth and since then had made her home with my eldest khala, Lubna, in Multan. Lubna Khala was married to a farmer turned tycoon. He had agricultural lands near Multan which he had converted into a chicken farming conglomerate. He was one of the biggest suppliers of poultry in the country and had diversified into the production of chicken feed and frozen chicken products. Lubna Khala and Shafiq Khalu lived close to the farm on an estate which also contained houses of Shafiq Khalu's three brothers and two sisters. After retirement from their various jobs, his brothers-in-law had joined Shafiq Khalu and his brothers in the chicken business.

Nani had borne, brought up, and married off six daughters but she was childlike in her enjoyment of life. She was tiny and becoming tinier, but was perpetually happy and full of pep, ready for adventure and never shy about trying something new. She was highly social and loved spending time with people...any people. She enjoyed living in Multan as she was within walking distance of so many families and had become a part of everyone's life. But, of course, her favorites were her grandchildren. She gave each one of us the impression that he/she was the one she loved most. Actually she had so much love to give that there was more than enough to go around.

I eagerly cleaned and readied Nadeem Bhai's room for Nani's arrival, and on the day itself put fresh flowers on her night table to welcome her. When I returned from college she was there! We hugged and kissed and I snuggled into her. Her head came up to my ear lobe but her heart was huge. The familiar fragrance of *motia* that emanated from her reminded me of all the wonderful times we had spent together.

At tea time the subject of my getting settled was inevitably discussed.

"It isn't as easy as I had hoped," said Ammi.

"It never is, *beta*," chuckled Nani. "You think you will never find a match and then suddenly out of the blue the perfect person appears. It will happen that way for Amna too."

I plugged my view. "And Nani, there is no hurry. I have three years more to go before I graduate."

"That's right, there is no need to be hasty, Rabia," Nani continued, suddenly turning serious. "Never make the decision in a hurry. It takes time to find a good match. I only had trouble with Azra. I got panicky about her and see what happened. Never a day passes that I don't regret having caused her sorrow. But, Allah has helped her and she has managed her life to perfection," Nani concluded, cheerful again.

Then she turned to me. "May I tell you a serious story? I promise no more sermons after this. After dinner we have to rope in your father and play Trumps. If I don't touch cards on a daily basis my health suffers." She ended with a grin.

"Of course, Nani. Even your lectures are fun." And Ammi and I directed our full attention at her.

"This is a story told to me by Shafiq's sister," Nani began, "and I will tell it as I remember Naheed telling it to me, in her words."

THE STORY OF THE TWO SISTERS

I first met Yasmeen and Nasreen when I was about ten years old, although they had been living only three houses down from us for years. In those days visiting even neighbors was a big deal, at least in our family. First, a servant had to be sent to check whether a visit from us was acceptable on that day and at that time. Next we sallied forth to execute the visit, which never exceeded more than forty-five minutes or an hour. During the visit the hosts plied us with good stuff to eat and drink and it was up to us to decline all that we were offered. Only after great insistence, and if our mother nodded imperceptibly at us, were we allowed to partake sparingly of the refreshments. One time my sister came home hungry from a lunch party because the hosts had not insisted enough that she help herself to the eats. Another time I was told that I had embarrassed the family by eating two slices of cake during a visit.

Yasmeen and Nasreen's parents were more modern. The sisters went to a coeducational school and ate their fill at our house when we became friends.

On their first visit they descended upon us in the middle of the afternoon without alerting us of their intention. It was the wrong time, of course. I was reading the Quran with the *maulvi sahib* and my mother was taking her afternoon siesta. The servant who answered the doorbell had no idea what to do. Finally my older sister cautiously woke my mother to ask her. Since the guests were already at the door they were allowed in. But they had to wait while I finished my day's lesson.

After that first time the sisters visited us several times a week. They just walked over when they liked, often even without receiving express permission from their mother, Auntie Firdous, as I started calling her.

The father of Yasmeen and Nasreen was a man absorbed in his own life. He was a bureaucrat and always had a look of suppressed irritation on his face. Either the office or the home was too much for him. All we saw was a person who never really looked at his daughters, let alone their friends. He lived in an invisible glass cage and if any noise was loud enough to impinge on his thoughts he turned toward it with a ferocious scowl. The culprit usually managed to skulk away without being scolded because he had only been heard but not noted as an actual person.

Auntie Firdous was a dream mother. She looked like a film star. Her hair was cut fashionably and was light brown in color. She was tall and slim and wore diaphanous saris which trailed behind her. But the best part was that she was always laughing and smiling. I felt joyful in her presence. In all the years that I visited their house there was never a rule that needed to be followed. Nasreen and Yasmeen liked coming over to our house. They said the eats were better. But I loved being in theirs. I could kick off my shoes and run barefoot inside the house and out. We could eat in between meals and we could yell and whoop it up even in the drawing room. Their house was paradise!

We met at least a couple of times a week for about a decade before we went our separate ways. I think Yasmeen and Nasreen liked the order and calm of our house, and I loved the liberty of theirs. Strangely, our mothers became friends too. They did not meet often but they appeared to enjoy each other's company when they did.

Yasmeen and Nasreen were so much a part of one another that I do not remember ever saying one name alone. Yet they were almost opposites in temperaments. Nasreen, the younger by a year, was a lot like her mother: happy, even-tempered, smiling and easy to please. Yasmeen was also full of fun but it was essential for her to win and have her own way. Being second, even to Nasreen, was unacceptable. She insisted she was older and so somehow more important. Yet sometimes she behaved like a baby to get what she wanted. I remember one summer vacation afternoon when I was visiting them, Yasmeen threw herself on the floor and writhed and sobbed as she insisted that she be allowed to go to Karachi to attend a cousin's wedding. Nasreen and I stood hugging the wall, shaken, as we witnessed this tantrum. Auntie Firdous was less affected. She must have seen such displays before. But Yasmeen did get her way and went off to Karachi triumphantly.

We went to different colleges when the time came. Yasmeen and Nasreen were sent to a Home Economics College to learn home crafts and I went on to do my B.A in History in another institution. Our friendship continued and now took on an added spice. Our families had started thinking of arranging marriages for us and there were always schemes afoot to meet prospective life partners.

I was the first to get married. This put a distance between us so I was not privy to how the matches were arranged for Yasmeen and Nasreen. Their joint wedding took place just after I had been married a year. They both seemed happy with the choice of grooms, and the wedding, which I attended, was well organized.

Now a great gulf opened in our relationships. We were not even in the same city for many years and only after a decade or so did my family and I return to Lahore.

By that time I had two children, both going to school, and a husband who was climbing the corporate ladder. Our evenings were busy socially and my days were full of housekeeping chores and the children. There was no time to look up old friends.

Quite by chance, at a lunch party hosted by the wife of my husband's colleague, I met Nasreen. She was radiant in a yellow chiffon sari with a printed cotton blouse. She had on lipstick and *surma* but hardly any other makeup. Yet her face glowed from inside. I was genuinely happy to see her and sat with her throughout the lunch to catch up on her news.

Nasreen was married to a professor at Punjab University and lived in university housing. Her daughters were almost the same ages as my children. The real story bubbled out of her when I asked her what her husband was like.

Her husband, Kazim, was an orphan with no close relatives except a sister, but with a host of friends. When they got married, Kazim took Nasreen straight to the small flat in which he lived. His friends had made a red carpet of rose petals all the way up the stairs and to their bedroom and the floor of the bedroom was also strewn with petals. The whole place was fragrant with love. She had never been given such importance, never even imagined such a welcome for herself. Her heart became tender and ready to love the person who was lavishing all this attention on her.

Kazim turned out to be a very caring and thoughtful husband in his quiet way. He thought of Nasreen's comfort and happiness before all else. Day by day Nasreen blossomed under his gaze. She reciprocated by loving Kazim back and caring for his every need. She knew what he wanted before he did and she could make him more comfortable than he could himself. Their mutual regard created such an atmosphere of warmth and adoration that they both flourished in it to become better people.

"We never fight or bicker, you know," Nasreen confided. "I just like doing what Kazim wants."

There was no mother-in-law to take exception to Nasreen having only daughters. Kazim wanted no more than two children and doted on his little girls. Nasreen was happy in Kazim's happiness.

They were not rich. Professors were notoriously low paid. But they lived within their means and saved a little. Nasreen did her own cooking and stitched all the girls' clothes. They led quiet lives. She had become a great reader over the years and she and her husband often read the same books together.

I returned after the lunch with much to think about. In my one decade of marriage I had rarely come across such compatibility and contentment and had certainly never encountered it in our own age group. It soothed me to spend time with Nasreen. Her life seemed to be uncomplicated, light and easy.

I had been of the opinion that my life was very good. Now I began to reexamine it. My husband was often too tired when he returned from work to ask about my day, let alone know of my needs instinctively. Pressed for time, we generally exchanged news about work and children in the car on our way to a social engagement. I made sure he had clean shirts in his closet and the food of his choice on the table. I considered that to be my role as a wife. He, on the other hand, rarely noticed what I ate or wore. But he was unfailingly polite, a good provider, a fond father. We seldom fought since our spheres of interest were so well defined. It was a good marriage but then, my face did not glow.

About a month later I met Yasmeen when Nasreen invited us both to a coffee morning. Nasreen's house was rather low beamed and drab, but spotlessly clean. Solid wood furniture from Kazim's parents' home dominated the drawing room. The walls were nearly bare and the tables had neat piles of books on them but no knick-knacks. A few large leafy plants made the room homey.

The most decorative piece in the room was Yasmeen. I could smell her perfume as I entered. She wore a bright red Thai silk *shalwar qameez* with a hand painted chiffon *dupatta* and perfectly matching designer shoes and handbag. Her manicure and pedicure were obviously freshly and expertly done. Yasmeen's long dark braid was gone and she now had auburn hair cut very stylishly. The resemblance to Auntie Firdous was marked except that Yasmeen had put on some weight and her lips were pulled down as if she was contending with an unpleasant smell.

After effusive greetings the exchange of news began. Yasmeen was married to a doctor, a surgeon, and there was no lack of money in her life. Her parents-in-law lived with them. Her husband, Naeem, was one of five siblings who all had large families and who all loved to spend time together.

Yasmeen had two sons. "I am not going to go on producing just because Naeem would like a daughter. I have already lost my figure and the stretch marks on my belly look like Niagara Falls. No sir, no more children for me," she said, waving her red-oval-tipped fingers in the air.

When they first got married, Yasmeen's husband had made much of her modern, 'western' ways since he came from a more conservative family. She could produce caramel custard and apple crumble for dessert while his family was still stuck in the *kheer* and *sivayan* rut. Her outfits were always color coordinated and her makeup flawless. She had novel ideas about decorating the house and laying the table for guests. For the doctor, all this was new and wonderful. His bride bowled him over. He told his mother and sisters that they should learn home-making from Yasmeen who knew everything!

Yasmeen felt she had won the lottery. She had always wanted to be best and now her husband was not only acknowledging her superiority but even advertising it.

Unfortunately the bubble soon burst. The doctor's mother and sisters remained silent; but it did not take long for Yasmeen's own ways to set the doctor's teeth on edge. While relating an anecdote to his friends, if he said it happened on Tuesday, she would set him right by pointing out it was really Monday night. If he quoted a couplet from Ghalib she reminded him the word was *"gham'* not *"dukh."*

When Yasmeen started to question Naeem's medical knowledge, the relationship soured in earnest. If Naeem talked about an interesting case in his clinic, she would question his diagnosis or even the need to operate. At first Naeem began second guessing himself. He became less confident in making decisions. Finally he decided not to share his day's activities with Yasmeen at all. So the couple talked less and less to each other. In company Naeem only spoke if Yasmeen was not around.

Yasmeen became lonely in the crowd of her in-laws. College friends had dispersed after marriage; Nasreen lived at quite a distance. She turned toward her children for solace. At the ages of eight and six they were neither the best looking nor at the top of their classes, poor babies. Yasmeen did not have much material with which to work.

Yasmeen did not say all this to me. I inferred it from her discourse and from silent winces on Nasreen's face. I also understood that Yasmeen was a very regular visitor at Nasreen's home. She must have felt at ease there since she was clearly richer and better dressed and because Nasreen was in the habit of deferring to her.

Over the next ten years we met many times, usually at Nasreen's house, for it had a special serenity. When Yasmeen was the hostess you could see she had gone to great lengths to create a perfect party. Such perfection took its toll in so many different ways that we went to her house rarely.

Time passed and we went our separate ways yet again.

About a dozen years later I was visiting Lahore when I heard from Nasreen that Yasmeen's husband was very ill. I made it a point to go to see them the next day.

Yasmeen met me at the door of her house. She was immaculately dressed, perhaps because I had called her earlier. Her hair and nails had been to a salon recently. She looked as gorgeous as always except for the shadows under her eyes and the more prominent droop of her mouth.

Dr. Naeem was propped up in a wheelchair and smiled when he saw me. He was skeletal and his clothes were hanging on him. I sat down and we started making small talk very laboriously. It was obvious that Yasmeen did not want to talk about Naeem's condition. After a while she left to supervise the tea trolley for me, even though I begged her not to go to any trouble.

When we were alone I asked the doctor how he really was. He told me calmly that he was very bad and that he would not last long. I wanted to know whether he was comfortable. Was there anything anyone could do for him?

At this he smiled ruefully and said. "Your friend is a djinn. She does everything better than anyone else can. Now she is taking care of me like a djinn. All that can be done is being done."

Yasmeen returned followed by a servant who pushed a well-laden tea trolley into the room. At about the same time one of Naeem's sisters arrived and the talk became general.

The next day I went to see Nasreen. Her husband had retired and they now led an even quieter life in a housing estate developed for university faculty. Both their girls were married. One lived in Dubai and one in the city.

I was surprised when Nasreen asked me how Naeem was doing since I had been planning on asking her the details of his illness. Reluctantly Nasreen told me that she almost never saw her sister. Apparently Yasmeen had taken exception at some point to the doctor's enjoyment of visits to Nasreen and Kazim. He liked the the gentle rhythm of their home. Yasmeen accused Nasreen of luring away her husband. Yasmeen's own visits had also become fewer till they finally ended when Naeem fell ill. Nasreen now just called occasionally and asked after Naeem as she did not want to strain the relationship any further.

Shortly thereafter, Naeem passed away. I attended the funeral as did Nasreen and Kazim. Before I left Lahore I visited Yasmeen once again. It was rather early in the morning and she was alone. Beautifully groomed and coiffed, she sat in her perfect drawing room.

Yasmeen shared her plans with me. She was closing the house and going to the U.S. where both her sons lived. She would give herself six months and if she liked living there, she would liquidate her assets in Lahore and move there permanently.

"There is nothing to keep me here anymore, and the United States is a whole new world," she said with a dazzling smile.

I asked her how she was feeling without Naeem after thirty-three years of togetherness. She thought for a moment and looked at me with a meaningful smile.

"Thirty-three years of togetherness it certainly was," she said. "But I asked Naeem once how he would define our marriage, and he said our relationship was the same as that of India and Pakistan."

I had sometimes questioned the quality of my marriage but as I returned from Yasmeen's house I had second thoughts. Like most marriages, ours had its ups and downs. But my husband often showed, in his undemonstrative way, that I mattered to him. After our children left to make their own lives, we had drawn closer. Gradually we even started to do more things together.

I never saw Yasmeen again. She did move to the U.S. and I heard later that she had become a very successful event manager among the Pakistani community and was also beginning to plan and sell exotic holiday packages to them.

———— ⟫«(◉)»⟪ ————

Nani ended and looked pointedly at me. It was a good story but how was I to make it my lodestar?

"You see, Amna, happiness isn't given to you on a golden platter. You have to make your own happiness." My grandmother then gave an audible sigh and said, "Enough, what's for dinner?"

During the following week I was on show again for some people, related somehow to Shafiq Khalu. The candidate looked good on paper. The young man was an architect and had just returned from the U.S. with a postgraduate degree. He was working with a big construction firm and earning well.

Nani came to help me choose what to wear. She had taken me shopping after her arrival to buy me a *jora* of my liking. I had bought a soft pink ensemble, dreaming of the vision presented by Sofia in the same color when she wore her *motia* earrings. I chose Nani's present to wear that evening. But I neither had makeup nor the requisite *motias*. Well....

The architect arrived with his parents and a younger brother. As I trundled the tea trolley into the room I was dazzled by four really handsome people. They certainly had good genes! I placed the trolley in front of my mother and went to sit on the vacant chair by the person whom I took to be the architect. The other young man looked far too callow.

As we made forced small talk, I realized how different my response to Saif had been. Since I was not the protagonist of that show, I had been easy and relaxed with him. That was probably why he had preferred me over Sofia, not my looks. I forced myself to relax and give a small smile to the architect before I asked him about his work. The regulation quarter hour passed amicably and when I got up to leave, my social aplomb was rewarded by a warm smile from him.

In the next few days we heard from the architect's family that they liked me. They sent a formal proposal and my mother countered with her usual "We need some time to consider" formula. Now both Saif and the architect were under consideration.

I was having a fine time. Nani was staying with us for a whole month and college was going great guns. Nani, Ghazala and I went out to eat, see movies and even to Clifton beach. Because of Nani's presence no one could say us nay and Ainee Auntie could enjoy a well-earned rest.

Ammi, on the other hand, was very busy. She had initiated detailed inquiries into the lives of Saif and the architect. All their connections, friends, relatives and acquaintances were quizzed about them. Their workplaces were checked out and their salaries verified. Nadeem Bhai was told to find out about Saif in England. Even their parents were put under the microscope. Were the fathers honest at work and good husbands at home? What were the temperaments of the mothers like, and how did they behave toward their in-laws? Most important, and most difficult, was to find out if Saif and the architect were good life-partner material. Ammi spent hours on the phone and reached out to even the most tenuous connections to further her quest.

Ammi estimated that it could take a year before a decision about my future was reached. But since the outcome was unknown and both the guys under consideration could turn out to be duds, the quest had to continue. That left me exactly at square one!

CHAPTER 9

In October my college had a talent show. I had not taken part in it the previous year because I was still getting my bearings. But this year I intended to participate. The fact that I had no talent was not going to be a deal breaker. I had seen last year's show and very few students had any outstanding skills. The talented ones took their art too seriously for their presentations to be fun, and the most applause was garnered by girls who were in it for laughs.

I spoke to Ghazala about a two-woman act I had in mind but she opted out. I wasn't surprised, for she suffered from the most intense case of stage fright. She was willing to help behind the scenes but I had to find another partner. I then approached Shahida, whom I had known only for a short while but whose sense of humor matched my own. She jumped at the idea and before we knew it we were deep in the planning stage, with Ghazala encouraging us at every step.

My plan was to relate two or three jokes on stage in each of which there were two speakers. It is a talent to tell a joke well. Shahida, Ghazala, and I started to go through old copies of Reader's Digest to locate good jokes. We checked out joke books from the college library and even pestered our fathers and uncles for any funny jokes or anecdotes they might know. We finally chose three jokes. Then Shahida and I started practicing the narration. Ghazala assigned the roles in each story and then she made us rehearse them till both Shahida and I were nearly sick to death of our lines.

Perhaps Ghazala was overly meticulous but on show day she was proved to be right. By the time Shahida and I began our jokes on stage we had our timing down pat. We received uproarious applause. No prizes came our way but we had ample reward in audience approval.

Even though everything was going my way at college it was not so at home. For months now I had been on exhibition. At first it was even a bit funny to be checked out by prospective mothers-in-law. But getting dressed for approval, pushing that silly tea trolley and then being on display for an endless stream of strangers was getting on my nerves. Sometimes I felt like sticking out my tongue at the guests and so ending the charade in an instant. One evening I cornered Ammi and told her how I felt.

"Ammi, the whole thing is fake. I am not the girl that they see, the butter-won't-melt-in her-mouth sort. And I am sure none of them is remotely like what they appear to be in the drawing room. Obviously we are all on our best behavior and never show our natural selves. So this method is bogus and useless and I don't want to be put on show any more." I was now in tears.

My mother heard me out and then beckoned me to sit by her. For some minutes she stroked my back.

"I understand what you are saying and you are right. But tell me what other method should we employ? Our religion and culture do not allow you to mix freely with the opposite sex. You go to an all-girls college. If we wait for you to finish your studies and start a job where you may be expected to meet young men you will find most of them are spoken for already." She paused and then, smiling at me, continued. "Even when you buy a pair of shoes you check out half a dozen stores, don't you? You don't buy the first pair you see. And shoes are only temporary possessions: they go out of fashion or become unsightly enough to be discarded. A husband is for life. For me there is no more important decision than to choose the right man for you. I cannot do it unless we see quite a few. And, my dear child, there comes a time in every girl's life when she attracts the most proposals. This seems to be your time. We cannot waste it. Who knows when the ideal young man will materialize?"

She gave me quick hug (surprising!) and a pat on my back.

"I am glad we had this talk," she concluded. "Now we understand each other."

Only to some extent! I did know that she was trying her best for my future. But I also knew Ammi's doggedness. She was going to do this job better than any mother in world history and in the process make my life miserable.

A curious thing happened the very next day when I had to wear my Ammi-approved turquoise *jora* and be ready for another group of hopefuls. This family was introduced to us by Khalid Chacha's mother-in-law. The family owned a pharmaceutical company and the young man in question had joined the family business after getting a masters in Chemistry. The parents, sister and various aunts and uncles had accompanied the chemist. Ammi had been told that a large contingent was coming and so the tea trolley was loaded. I was pushing it very carefully, so as not to cause any disarray to Ammi's arrangement. By the drawing room door I paused to straighten a plate. Suddenly, I heard Ammi speak in a slightly raised voice.

"Well, then, this is the wrong house for you. We don't fulfill dowry demands."

I decided to eavesdrop further. Ammi's tone was so final that I was unsure whether I and the trolley would be on call.

"Sister," a male voice said, "Hajra Apa has just told you our tradition. We are not making demands. In our family, brides bring all the household goods and fifty *tolas* of gold with them."

"I am so glad that you told us of your expectations right away," my father said politely. "I think you should get your son married in your own family where no explanations will be needed and all your requirements will be met."

I peeked through the door jamb and saw that both my parents were standing up. Willy-nilly the guests stood up and made their way out. My parents remained silent till they were at the door and then said *Khuda Hafiz* to them very cordially!

I carefully turned the trolley round and wheeled it to the kitchen. I was so proud of my parents. We had a veritable feast that day. Ammi called Azra Khala and family over to help us finish the eats.

The next day an old friend of Ammi's from her college days came over with her bhabi. They had come armed with a whole bunch of test results and doctor's prescriptions to show to my father. They wanted to get a second opinion about the treatment of the bhabi's mother. Ordinarily visits to our home with the aim of getting Abba's medical advice were ruthlessly discouraged. Anyone who needed to see Abba professionally had to go to the hospital or his private clinic. Ammi and Abba felt the house was sacrosanct. But Ammi had allowed this friend to come to the house because the patient was a widow in straitened circumstances and my mother did not have the heart to refuse her.

The medical papers were kept safely to the side and Ammi promised to call and let them know what my father had to say the very next day. Meanwhile, I was asked to get the tea. I trundled my old friend, the tea trolley, into the room but this time with a free and easy feeling of being there just as the daughter of the house. I poured the tea and served the two guests cake and samosas from the trolley. The samosas were of my doing courtesy of Mrs. Bhimjee. When my mother's friend praised them, Ammi told her that I had made the samosas which made the bhabi look at me again.

"What a nice child, *Mashallah*. Is she engaged?"

"Not yet. But we are looking for a suitable boy for her. Do you have someone in mind?"

"We will certainly keep Rabia's daughter in mind, won't we?" Ammi's friend looked at her bhabi and then addressed Ammi again. "Don't delay in getting the child married off. The quicker the better! Parents go on refusing proposal after proposal in the hopes of getting better and better ones and finally the girl becomes too old and they have to settle for some man they would not even have spoken a word to earlier on. So my advice is to be quick in getting her settled."

Oh! Wow, I thought disgustedly, another one cast in the same mold as my mother!

"No, no," said the mild-mannered bhabi, suddenly quite animated, "never be in a hurry when making such a big decision. You are not choosing glass bangles for her but a groom. Her whole life depends on your decision. The last thing to do is to be precipitate in this matter."

My mother smiled and tried to assure both her visitors that she was neither going to be over fussy nor in a rush to get me off her hands. But the bhabi wasn't done. The button of a pet peeve seemed to have been pushed.

"No, no, Rabia Apa. I am serious. Take your time in choosing a groom for your daughter. She is such a sweet child, treasure her and make the decision for her marriage only after great deliberation."

Ammi tried to say something but the bhabi went on.

"I will tell you a story about undue urgency in marriages. Then perhaps you will understand what I mean." And she proceeded to tell the following story.

The Story of Hasty Marriages

She was my grandmother's maid. I didn't know her name because she was simply called Shaddo's mother. When I met her she was old, at least seventy, and died not many years thereafter. She epitomized the firm belief that marriages should be solemnized speedily whatever the cost.

Her own marriage was a disaster. There was no record of any joyful interlude, even at the beginning. The story began in Delhi, in undivided India, where she had three children and a husband who had become an opium addict. He had stopped earning and in fact stole whatever he could from the house to feed his habit. Even the pots and pans in the kitchen were not safe.

In desperation Shaddo's mother decided to decrease the mouths to feed in the family by marrying off her eldest daughter, Ameera. She had been affianced to a cousin many years earlier. When Shaddo's mother approached the fiancé's father to push for an early marriage the prospective groom was still studying at Aligarh University and Ameera was fourteen.

"If you count the months in the womb," Shaddo's mother would interpose.

The fiancé and his father declined the offer of early marriage. They explained that the university degree had to be completed first.

For Shaddo's mother speed was of the essence and so she called off the marriage in a huff.

A neighbor of Shaddo's mother who knew about the impoverished circumstances of the family put forward her own brother as a candidate for Ameera's hand. The brother was pushing forty and quite illiterate but was tall, strong and had a sleek, well-fed look. The real drawback was that Qutubuddin, the prospective groom, was averse to working. He had never held down a job for longer than a few weeks and it was his sister who shouldered the duty of keeping his sleek look intact by serving his favorite foods at lunch, when the long suffering brother-in-law was out of the house.

All Shaddo's mother saw in this offer was a way to lighten her own burden. She agreed to the match if the wedding could take place within a week. Since no one could see any reason for delay, the wedding took place on the following Friday. Qutubuddin, who had been turned down by scores of mothers whose demand was that their daughter's husband should earn enough to feed and clothe the wife, suddenly acquired a young, pleasant-faced, literate bride.

How did the marriage work? Qutubuddin had never broken a sweat at work and did not want to begin doing so now just because he was married. Gradually it could be observed that Qutubuddin's sister started developing the same sleek look as her brother. Since the wedding she had much more time to rest on the string bed in the courtyard. The only interruption was an occasional reminder to Ameera to take care of the family's laundry before she started lunch, or to clean up after one of the children who had soiled himself. As for Ameera, it was her duty to make herself useful. She and Qutubuddin were given a small room off the kitchen to live in and food thrice a day. A bit of housework killed no one, the sister felt, and Ameera was young and strong.

Poor Ameera did not remain young or strong for long. Time took care of the former and never-ending miscarriages of the latter.

Qutubuddin saw no reason to have children. He was happy with his life as it was: a place to sleep, good food and a minimum amount of responsibility. It was Ameera who hankered after a baby. She had started stitching tiny clothes when she first became pregnant. Having no money to buy fabric she had resorted to subterfuge. She purposely ripped her husband's *shalwar* in the wash, listened to the inevitable scolding patiently and then, while her husband snored after a meal of *alu gosht* and *naan*, unpicked all the seams of the ruined *shalwar*, flattened the fabric and began her stitchery.

Ameera kept the baby clothes through two miscarriages. Then she gave them away as gifts to the lucky neighbors who had live births. This opened the door to her real talent, sewing. Her baby clothes were appreciated by all and since babies were always being born in the community she got a steady stream of orders from mothers and grandmothers.

Ameera loved creating the tiny dresses, bibs, sheets, towels. She reveled in the touch of brand new fabric. Soon she began asking her clients for skeins of silk and every article of baby clothing bloomed with exquisite embroidery.

After the day's work was done, the pots and pans washed and the last child put to bed, she would come to her small room and sit on the floor leaning against the wall. By that time Qutubuddin would be in deep sleep, digesting his dinner. She would then pull out the latest order and begin working. As she set each perfect stitch in place with her work-roughened fingers, her fatigue melted away. When she held up a completed garment she almost forgot her own childlessness.

Even though Ameera's clients were poor like herself she did get paid. Sometimes she was given a piece of fabric, sometimes real money. She hoarded and hid every coin she received, even though she had no idea what she would do with it.

Year after year passed by and then suddenly Ameera heard that Pakistan was being established. The information washed off her leaving no mark. It was not her concern. Her life was a round of cooking, cleaning and child care on the one hand and listening to reprimands and insults on the other. Some nights she had to endure the fumbling and groping of her husband and every so often she had to go through agony as she lost another child. Her only solace was creating the most delectable baby clothes night after night.

The time came when Pakistan could not be ignored any more. As she sat in her room making a border of tiny pink flowers on a blanket, the noise in the street outside rose to a peak and the door of the house was rapped on loudly. Her husband's brother-in-law opened the door, Ameera heard raised and excited voices and then the sister-in-law came into her room, barefoot.

Conditions had become bad, she explained. The government had announced that Muslims could not be guaranteed safety in their homes. As a protective measure they were asked to go to Purana Qila early the next morning. They could bring only the barest essentials with them.

Ameera put away the blanket with the pink flowers. She went to the children's rooms and took out two changes of clothing for each child and tied them up in an old towel. She then went to the kitchen and made a large stack of *chappatis* and boiled all the potatoes and eggs in the house. These too she tied up in a square of cloth. She then put her husband's clothes in a bundle together with the only other *shalwar qameez* she possessed. The cache of money she had saved she put in a pouch and hid between her breasts. She was now ready for Pakistan.

The following morning her husband's sister wept and wailed as she left behind all she owned. The children huddled around the silent Ameera, in a fog of bewilderment. The brother-in-law locked the house carefully and led them all to the trucks waiting to take them away. Qutubuddin followed, scratching his armpit, no less puzzled than the children. He had not even been able to finish his breakfast tea.

They never came back to the house again. Even though the sister and her husband wrangled with the authorities every day, conditions never improved enough for them to be allowed to return to their home. About a month later they were all herded into trains and sent off to Pakistan.

That is when the nightmare began in earnest. As darkness fell the train was stopped, power was cut and mobs of Sikhs and Hindus fell on the hapless passengers. They were armed with`kirpans and *lathis* and knives and they knew how to use them. When day broke the train was still, silent and slick with blood.

But everyone was not dead. From under bodies sporting garish wounds, crawled out a dozen or so people who were still alive. Among them were Ameera, her husband and his sister. None of the children survived, nor did their father.

There was no time to mourn or look for a loved one. A small contingent of the Indian Army arrived on the scene, better late than never, and led them along the tracks for the few miles that separated them from Pakistan.

Ameera and her family settled in Karachi. They were given one of the aluminum sheds specially put up for the refugees who were pouring across the border. Qutubuddin tried to find work but the new milieu puzzled him and he even lost his sleek look. His sister was a ghost of her former self. She took over the role of Ameera in the new country and did all the household chores while Ameera sewed everything from baby clothes to burkas day and night. Pakistan gave Ameera the status and importance of being the bread winner.

That was Ameera's story, but even after her hasty marriage, Shaddo's mother's financial problems did not improve. So Shaddo's mother decided it was time to marry off the younger daughter, Shaddo, as well. Ten months after Ameera's wedding, Shaddo was married to a middle aged, lecherous, philanderer whose only qualification was that he did not want a dowry. The nubile body of a 13-year-old was enough for him to agree to marriage.

As soon as she got rid of her second daughter, Shaddo's mother put on her *burka*, clasped the hand of her 10-year-old son and went to the house of my grandmother, who, she had been told, was looking for a maid.

So Shaddo's marriage took place and forthwith the husband, Abid Ali, infected her with syphilis. She endured the suffering of hell. Fortunately, newly discovered drugs worked their wonder and she was cured...cured but barren. At fifteen Shaddo became more mature than her own mother. She demanded compensation for her pain and loss. Abid Ali was made to feel shame. Also, he was increasingly unwell and too weak to argue. He needed to be looked after by his wife. So Shaddo decreed that he would never be allowed access to her body again, and that he would finance her education. By the time Pakistan became a fact she was a full-fledged homeopathic doctor. She migrated to Pakistan with her ailing husband and, in the brand new country where every service was in short supply, she established a lucrative medical practice.

Shaddo's mother worked for my grandmother in Delhi and then in Karachi and kept Sultan, her son, with her. Her husband had first been abandoned when she went into service and later the melee of Partition swirled him into oblivion. Shaddo's mother spent every *rupee* of her salary on Sultan's needs and schooling. He was a good child, obedient and obliging, but not very bright.

He reached Karachi as a tall teenager who had two more years to complete high school. When he finally passed the Matric exam, Shaddo's mother smiled. Sultan got a job with the Post and Telegraph Department as a postman and began to earn a regular salary. It was time he got married. His mother could brook no delay.

Poor Sultan was no beauty. He was thin and tall and so emaciated that his body at rest was a perfect figure 'S.' He had a huge Adam's apple in his thin neck and its movement, as he swallowed in his shyness, was enough to distract attention from his homely face.

Shaddo's mother decreed that he marry her cousin's daughter, Rani, who was a couple of years older than Sultan and had been left on the shelf because of the upheaval of Partition. In her inimitable style Shaddo's mother did not spend a second to assess whether Rani was right for Sultan. There was nothing obviously wrong with Rani, so, according to Shaddo's mother, she was right.

And in fact nothing was wrong with Rani. She was the reigning belle of four or five *mohallas* and was a feast for the eyes. Tall, slightly plump with a tiny waist and luscious grapefruit like breasts which seemed to be on the point of spilling out of her clothing, Rani had a walk which alone was enough to break male hearts at every swaying step. She knew how to flutter her eyelids, and when, how to make the perfect moue, and exactly how to strike a pose to greatest effect. This bombshell was married to poor hapless Sultan, and people held their breath waiting for the impending disaster.

Nothing happened for more than four years except for the arrival of two children, a boy and a girl. We didn't know whether all was well with the household during this time because Shaddo's mother had left my grandmother's employment and moved in with her son who had been given a small house by his department. Just twice did Shaddo's mother visit my grandmother in these four years. Each time she came with a box of sweets to announce the birth of a grandchild. All was well, she insisted, and so returned to her son's house.

Misfortune did befall the family as expected, though from a direction that no one had imagined. One evening when Sultan returned from work he fell ill and the next day he was dead. While on his rounds, he had caught cholera when he ate a plate of *haleem* from a push cart. Rani cried and mourned and Shaddo's mother, who had not cried through her husband's addiction, her daughters' miseries, or her own relegation to servitude, cried too. The day after the funeral, Rani came out of her room in a bright blue *shalwar qameez* and with a cloth bag stuffed with her things. The children could be heard whimpering in her room. Rani went up to Shaddo's mother who was making tea in the kitchen.

"I am going," she said and walked out of the door.

Shaddo's mother struggled up from the low stool in front of the fire and ran after her. Rani did not look back. Shaddo's mother watched as she walked out on the road and went away with a man on a motor bike, a blur of blue. That was the last that anyone saw of Rani. Shaddo's mother went back to work for my grandmother, this time holding the hands of both her grandchildren.

When the boy turned five, Dr. Shaddo took away Sultan's son to educate him. Chammi, the daughter, stayed behind. Though ill and old, Abid Ali could not to be trusted with a seven-year-old girl living under his roof.

Shaddo's mother refused to send Chammi to school so my grandmother insisted she be taught reading and writing and the Quran at home. The lady who came to read the Quran aloud to my grandmother was asked to spend a half hour with Chammi every day.

Chammi was a good natured, chubby girl with dazzling white teeth and fat cheeks that shone like polished apples. She was often seen humming under her breath as she played with twigs and wind-blown flowers in the rear garden. Told to mind her letters, Chammi complied with good humor, but the lessons did not take. Chammi was not bright. After several years of struggle, she could read simple sentences in Urdu but she never did manage to complete the recitation of the Quran.

As soon as Chammi turned eleven, Shaddo's mother confined her to the room that they shared. This was a pokey, windowless cubicle all of eight feet by eight. Their bed rolls rested against the wall during the day and two small shelves held their other belongings. Chammi had to spend the entire day and night in this sterile prison. She had nothing to occupy her except, perhaps, her dreams. Three times Shaddo's mother came in with their meals which they ate together. At night they slept on the floor, side by side, in the center of the room under the fan. Nothing my grandmother said budged Shaddo's mother from her resolve of keeping Chammi virtuous by keeping her jailed.

As was her wont, Shaddo's mother started thinking of Chammi's marriage by the time the girl turned thirteen. My grandmother's vociferous objections were overruled. The child was promised to a 35-year-old paunchy clerk who brought boxes of sweets every time he visited. He was a 'government servant' and so thought to be a catch. Shaddo's mother took the boxes of sweets to be proof of his good nature and generosity. My grandmother interviewed the government clerk and failed him on every count. But Shaddo's mother was adamant. So the inevitable took place and Chammi went away with the clerk.

Shortly after this wedding, Shaddo's mother started to ail and so retired from service. Less than six months later Dr. Shaddo came to apprise us of her mother's demise. Mercifully, she died before she had to bear more sorrow.

Chammi escaped from her jail only to be used and abused by her fat clerk and his family. None of us knew the story of all that befell her, but before the first anniversary of the wedding, she died of burns when the stove burst in the kitchen. No one else in the house was harmed.

We did not know the fate of Chammi's brother either. After the death of Shaddo's mother and of Chammi we lost touch with the family. Perhaps Sultan's son was educated, gainfully employed and happily married. It was possible, since poor Shaddo's mother had no hand in matchmaking for him.

———————◦《◦》◦———————

The bhabi ended her story and looked around triumphantly. Silence reigned. Then my mother cleared her throat and reassured the bhabi once again that no decision would be made in a hurry.

That evening Zahid Bhai came over. He had just sent off all the requisite applications and paperwork to the UK for his postgraduate training and was feeling relieved and happy. Both he and my father spent time studying the medical papers left behind by Ammi's friend. After dinner I collared Zahid Bhai.

"Zahid Bhai, I am scared of getting married. It seems to end in disaster, always. You should have heard the stories I heard today." And then I recounted the stories of Shaddo's mother's family to poor Zahid Bhai.

"Don't let these stories frighten you," Zahid Bhai said. "Rabia Mumani is too smart to make such mistakes in your case. Just look around you, your aunts and uncles have happy marriages. So your marriage will be good too, *Inshallah*."

"Do you think so?" I asked hopefully, already a little more composed. Zahid Bhai continued to talk to me for a while longer and allayed my fears with his patient counseling.

I held his hand in mine. "Thank you. I don't know what I will do when you leave for England."

He patted my head, smiled and left.

CHAPTER 10

Poor Ainee Auntie's mother fell seriously ill and had to be admitted into hospital. It was decided that Ghazala would come to stay with us for the duration so that Ainee Auntie could give her full attention to her mother. As the saying goes, every cloud has a silver lining, so even though her grandmother was unwell Ghazala was over the moon. So was I. Most days we asked our friends, Shahida and Shaheen, to come over after college and spent time giggling, doing each other's hair, and chatting. It was bliss.

But as another saying goes, nothing lasts forever. My two khalas who lived abroad signaled their imminent arrival. One would stay with Azra Khala and one with us. Ghazala and I accelerated our revelries, knowing that once there was a khala in residence we would have to behave ourselves.

These two khalas lived abroad and I hardly knew them. Farida Khala was the one immediately before Ammi and she lived in Saudi Arabia with her husband. She was two years older than my mother and got married two years before her. Since her husband worked for Aramco she went to Saudia, and because of high Saudi salaries, immediately became rich. When she came home on leave she upstaged all her sisters because she could afford what was beyond the grasp of her siblings, married as they were to struggling young men. She missed no opportunity to brag about her luxurious life in Dhahran and about all her foreign trips.

Nani had told me all this in her usual candid way to explain why no one quite liked Farida Khala. Farida Khala had never hesitated to point out that nothing could compare with what she was used to in Saudia. Azra Khala and Ammi who lived in Karachi were her chief targets. What they wore, what they ate, how they lived and how they brought up their offspring were all wrong. She covered her nose at the smells in Karachi and complained bitterly about the heat in a city where air-conditioning was not common.

Gradually the financial status of Ammi's sisters improved as their husbands became senior in their professions; or, in the case of Azra Khala, when she struck gold in her business. Now Farida Khala had nothing to brag about except for all the high end things she could buy. Even in this, she had tough competition from Tahira Khala and her brood.

Farida Khala had two sons who were, of course, handsome and clever, and both had been sent to the U.S. after high school. They shattered their mother's dreams when they married American girls after graduation. Farida Khala had been scheming for years about bringing them to Pakistan on a royal tour to select consorts for them. Instead, she was left with the necessity of making lame excuses about why they got married to foreigners. Nani said that after her boys' marriages, Farida Khala drastically curtailed her visits to Pakistan.

The other khala who lived abroad was Nusrat Khala, Ammi's youngest sister. She had turned out to be the beauty of the family and got married many years before Azra Khala, who was older. But Nusrat Khala's early nuptials did not augur happiness (Hmm, shades of Shaddo's mother?).

She was married to Hassan Khalu who was almost as young as she was. He was the only child of a family settled in Manchester. The father was a civil engineer and the mother was a martinet. I had never met the mother-in-law but all stories started with "Poor Nusrat" and detailed her mother-in-law's perfidies. She ruled both her husband and her son and saw no reason to change her ways with the imported daughter-in-law. Nusrat Khala was easy prey as she had a sweet disposition and very mild manners. She did not even try to defy her mother-in-law, far away as she was from her family and married to a mama's boy into the bargain. She just became a doormat to her new family and got trampled underfoot.

It took Nusrat Khala five years to get pregnant, during which time she heard every cutting remark ever invented about her inability to conceive. Her only contact with her family was by mail. But she had to let her mother-in-law read every letter that came to her from Pakistan and every letter she wrote in reply. Nani always had tears in her eyes when she spoke of Nusrat Khala.

"When I saw her, seven years after her marriage, on her first visit to Pakistan, she wasn't pretty anymore."

Nusrat Khala bore all this bravely but what shattered her was the death of her son. Obviously the son, born after nearly six years of marriage, was precious for all. For Nusrat Khala he became the only one who was totally hers. In her own quiet way she loved him intensely. With each passing year her love deepened. And then, on his way back from school one day, he was beaten to death by skinheads. He was thirteen years old.

Nusrat Khala went into a deep depression. Nobody thought she would recover. Even her mother-in-law was shaken out of her complacency. After many years of medication and psychiatric help Nusrat Khala found her way out of the vortex of her misery. But she remained fragile and nervous.

Now Nusrat Khala was coming with Hassan Khalu to stay with us for a week on their way to Nani in Multan. Ghazala and I were given a serious lecture by my mother about respecting Nusrat Khala's need for silence and harmony. Her timings were not to be questioned and we had to make sure her stay was pleasant in every way.

When Ghazala and I returned from college the following Wednesday, Nusrat Khala and Hassan Khalu had already arrived and were resting in Nadeem Bhai's room. We tiptoed to my room and carefully shut the door before we uttered a word. In the evening, only when we heard movement and voices from outside did we go to greet the guests.

Everyone was having tea as we quietly joined them. Ammi introduced us and we mumbled our salaams in undertones. I darted a quick glance at Nusrat Khala and found her smiling at me. She was as thin as a pin and dressed in outdated clothes. Her hair was sparse and pulled back in a tight knot at the nape of her neck. The clothes and hair did nothing to enhance her looks but she had a sweet expression and a gentle manner. There was not a trace left of the earlier beauty of which I had heard so much.

Hassan Khalu was so average in his looks and had such a plain and unmemorable face that if he had not been an engineer he could have taken up a life of crime quite profitably...no eyewitness would ever be able to describe him to the police. When Nadeem Bhai had gone to visit them in Manchester he had written that Hassan Khalu was 'normal.' Now I understood what he meant. Halfway through tea Abba came in and greeted the guests with his usual hearty sincerity which petered out in the face of a colorless response from Hassan Khalu and a sweet but mournful smile from Nusrat Khala. It was going to be a long week!

A little later Azra Khala brought Farida Khala, the other overseas guest, to meet us all. Azra Khala entered in her inimitable style: loud and overpowering and clad in flame pink paired with a venomous green. Farida Khala followed her in a cloud of expensive perfume. She was tall, with a perfect figure and dressed at the height of fashion in a very becoming shade of brown which offset her auburn coiffure perfectly. If you didn't see her face she could pass for age twenty. But her face told another tale. There were deep wrinkles from her nose to the corners of her mouth which decidedly drooped downwards. And there were dark bags under her eyes. Ghazala and I were met with hugs from Azra Khala and appraising looks from Farida Khala. We escaped before getting corralled into the inane conversation reserved for young, unmarried girls like us.

A few days later Ammi arranged a dinner for her visiting sisters. Since Ainee Auntie's mother had recovered and returned home, it was Ghazala's last day at our house. I helped to pack her suitcase, sad to part but happy in the knowledge that we would still be seeing each other every day.

All Ammi's parties were beautifully orchestrated and this was no different. The drawing room was decked with flowers, the hosts (we!) were well dressed and gracious, the menu was carefully chosen, and the food was a feast for the eyes as well as the palate. Ammi did all this out of habit, I thought, because the British guests noticed nothing and the Saudi visitor found fault with most things. None of the chairs in the drawing room was good for Farida Khala's back, the food was too highly spiced, Coca-Cola had Jewish origins and should not be served in Muslim homes, and was Ammi still using her trousseau crockery? Ammi and Abba let the criticism pass over them like a soft breeze as they smiled with diplomatic grace.

I suddenly became Farida Khala's target after dinner.

"Is your girl engaged, Rabia?" Farida Khala asked. Had she forgotten my name?

"Not yet. Why, do you have someone in mind?"

"Well, a friend of mine is looking for a girl for her son, but she wants one who is beautiful. So that's out. Can't you find someone in the family for her? Your girl is nothing out of the ordinary, though better than her friend, so you can't expect too much."

Ghazala and I stole a look at each other and nearly choked with pent up mirth.

Calmly Ammi said, "We are getting a lot of proposals for Amna, *Mashallah*. You needn't worry about her."

"But there is nothing wrong with looking within the family," interjected Nusrat Khala.

Everyone looked at her in surprise since she almost never spoke except in response to a question.

"There is no reason to dismiss the whole family out of hand. Who knows? Our Amna might even be interested in someone in the family." She gave me a sad smile. Everyone else turned to look at me too. Not knowing how to respond, I held my peace.

"No, Nusrat. If that were so Amna would have told me," Ammi replied gently.

"No, Rabia Apa, sometimes you find out only when it is too late."

More speculative glances turned toward me while I sat like a statue. Ghazala surreptitiously patted my hand in support.

"Hassan, please tell everyone the story of your mother's cousin and her son," Nusrat Khala said to her husband.

Hassan Khalu cleared his throat and began the story dutifully. He turned out to be a superb raconteur and all of us were spellbound.

The Story of the Slighted Sister

Kaneez Fatima woke up that morning with a premonition of disaster. It took her no more than thirty seconds to remember the cause. Her son was leaving for Lahore in a few hours. Her heart sank to her toes.

As soon as she finished her morning ablutions she hurried to the kitchen to oversee Munir's last breakfast. Then quickly she bit her tongue and said under her breath, "God forbid it is his last breakfast. May he have a long life, *Inshallah.*"

Kaneez Fatima shooed the maid out of the kitchen and sat down to make Munir's breakfast herself. In no time, it seemed, the breakfast was cooked and eaten, the *tonga* loaded and her son on the way to the railway station. She stood by the door till even the dust of the *tonga* was not visible any more. Then with head held high she walked back to her room.

Munir was her only child, for after Munir she never conceived again. In her heart, she always blamed the maladroit village midwife and also her own husband for not making arrangements to take her to the town only thirteen miles away. But she never uttered a word of blame. She knew her husband's limitations and appearances had to be kept up. She just wrapped her existence around little Munir and forgot about everything else.

Munir became all that Kaneez Fatima could wish for. He grew sturdy and tall and absorbed everything that he was taught like a sponge. The Quranic verses that she recited to him, the Urdu and English alphabets and numbers that she drummed into him and later the books that she left lying around were all mastered by little Munir with no effort. He went through school like a knife through butter and at the age of fifteen he sat his Matric exam and was placed third in the province.

Kaneez Fatima understood that Munir had to leave the village. She wanted him to conquer the world; to do what no one else had ever done before. Staying in the village was not an option. It would certainly not be seemly for him to take over his father's village grocery store and stagnate. But, Kaneez Fatima looked at the heavens, was there no other alternative than to send him to that smug and supercilious hussy in Lahore?

Kaneez Fatima came from a merchant family settled in Lahore. They had left the village early on to look for greater opportunities and had found a niche in Lahore in the egg business. Initially Kaneez Fatima's great grandfather collected eggs from the nearby villages on his bicycle and supplied them to a shop in Chauburji. As the business expanded the bicycle was fitted with a large box to accommodate the increasing number of eggs. Within his lifetime the great grandfather had bought a horse drawn vehicle to transport the constantly growing number of eggs to Lahore. It was not only his business acumen and hard work but also his honesty and promptness in paying his illiterate clients and his empathy for their problems that spurred on his business.

By the time Kaneez Fatima was born the family had become affluent. The egg business had grown to such proportions that every egg sold in Lahore passed directly or indirectly through the hands of her family. Her only brother became the first in the family to go to college. Even she and her sisters were sent to school. She had got a first division in Matric. But then, like her older sisters, she was betrothed and married off. It was the tradition to marry within the family and so her khala's son was chosen to be her spouse. Majid was a college graduate and, as the only son, he was set to inherit his father's grocery store. He would be based in the village but that was not an obstacle to the match.

So Kaneez Fatima got married and moved to the village. Her in-laws were good, honest people and she soon adjusted to the bucolic routine. But it was her husband whom she found to be an enigma at first and a disappointment for the rest of her life. He was soft spoken and considerate toward her. But his main interest was writing poetry. He spent his day at the store with a vague look in his eyes, polite to all but absent in essence. In the evening while her father-in-law did the accounts and filled in order forms for the required goods, he sat with a pencil in his hand and an abstracted look on his face jotting down a few words from time to time. Being young and healthy he did have physical interest in Kaneez Fatima but she was doubtful if he ever really heard what she said.

The daughter of energetic entrepreneurs, she was full of schemes for expanding the store and opening another one in the neighboring village that would become Majid's sole responsibility. Majid sat through her lectures and never volunteered a response. Slowly she also became less enthusiastic about business. A pattern of silence emerged between the couple which only deepened with the passing away of Majid's parents.

Kaneez Fatima learned to leave Majid to his own thoughts. The store had to be managed and manned but for the rest he could spend his time as he wished. He withdrew to his parents' room, only visiting her at night occasionally, and continued to provide a reasonable if not ample living. His room filled up with books, papers, and his own manuscripts.

Kaneez Fatima found she was content. Her life was complete because of Munir. It was rarely that she wished for more money to spend, and then only to buy the newest gadget for her son. In the village she was among the well-to-do and her son was taller, healthier and cleverer than all the other little boys. She was the queen of her house and lived a life so free of constraints that she was envied by most of her neighbors. When daughters got married their mothers hoped they would have lives like Kaneez Fatima's... free and independent to make their own decisions.

Into this life of measured rhythms came a letter from Lahore like a bolt of thunder. Kaneez Fatima's brother, Asif, had written to say that he wanted to come to the village for some business deal and stay with his sister. His wife would also accompany him. Kaneez Fatima was thrilled and apprehensive at the same time. Asif, married at that time for ten years, had fallen in love with a classmate and after an initial resistance by his parents the match had been accepted, not the least because the bride was the daughter of a senior bureaucrat who was very warm in the pocket. So Asif and

Shehla were married and now, for the first time, they were coming to visit Kaneez Fatima. She was determined to put on the best show for them. She may not be rich like them but she did not want to be taken for a backward provincial either.

She had the house cleaned till it sparkled. Majid was evicted from his parent's room, which was then made ready for Asif and his bride. The bed was made up with Kaneez Fatima's best trousseau bedding. Heavily embroidered table cloths were spread on the side tables and were held down with beaten brass vases sporting tight bouquets of real flowers. Kaneez Fatima knew better than to decorate her house with faux blooms.

Kaneez Fatima did not stop there. She sent her servant to town to get ingredients for the dishes which were favorites in her parents' house. The menu for the two days that Asif was going to spend in the village would in no way differ from what he was used to at home.

Finally Asif and Shehla arrived and were met at the door by an effusive Kaneez Fatima and a silent, but amiable, Majid. Munir was at school but returned soon after and was immediately presented to the visitors. And that is when it all started to go wrong. Asif and Shehla, too much involved in themselves to be really interested in a school boy, patted Munir's head perfunctorily and continued talking. Kaneez Fatima was first taken aback and then blazingly angry at her sister-in-law. This woman, dressed in such tight clothes and with the flimsiest of *dupattas*, who had produced nothing but a sickly girl child in ten years of marriage, this woman had the temerity to ignore Munir! She was sure poor Asif would have liked to show more affection to his brilliant nephew instead of nonchalantly handing the boy a Rs. 500 note, but he did not dare to do so in front of his wife.

The situation got worse at lunch when Shehla hardly ate at all. Kaneez Fatima presented her with dish after dish but she only took a dollop of yoghurt and ate it with plain white rice.

"Why, *Dulhan*, what is the matter? You are not eating. I have had everything especially cooked just like in my mother's house in Lahore so that it is familiar to you."

Before Shehla could answer, Asif guffawed loudly.

"Oh! Apa! Shehla could never eat our mother's food. It was so spicy and oily. Since she passed away we eat simple, light dishes and salads. Don't you see my paunch has disappeared?"

Kaneez Fatima looked at her brother in silence. Can people change so much?

After lunch Shehla went to rest and Asif left to keep his business appointment. Kaneez Fatima said her prayers and then retired to her room where she nursed her grudges. Her son was given no importance and her food was pronounced to be inedible. Was there more to come?

Of course there was. At tea time Shehla emerged from the room holding a handkerchief to her nose. She came to the table and sat there looking ill.

"What is the matter, *Dulhan*?" Kaneez Fatima asked.

"Nothing. But the smell of all these buffaloes is giving me a headache. As we were driving to your house I must have seen thousands of buffaloes of all ages, and miles of walls covered with drying dung cakes. The smell of the animals and their dung is so odious."

Kaneez Fatima could think of nothing to say. In the villages of Punjab, buffaloes were desirable possessions. They represented people's wealth. Nobody got a headache because of them.

She made a cup of tea, passed it to Shehla and waved a hand invitingly toward the accompanying snacks. Shehla shuddered delicately, shook her head and gingerly sipped her tea.

"Oh, no! This is sweet" Shehla grimaced. "I take my tea without sugar." Kaneez Fatima pursed her lips and made a fresh cup for Shehla.

For breakfast the next day Kaneez Fatima discarded the idea of *parathas* and eggs. She sent the servant to town to get bread and jam. She could not bear any more rejections. Munir and Majid had eaten and left by the time the guests emerged from their room. Asif looked worried and Shehla looked tired.

"Did you two have a good night's rest?" Kaneez Fatima asked.

"Well, Apa, Shehla is not used to *razais*. She has allergies. At home we now use only blankets at night. We did put your *razai* as far away from her as possible but she has developed a sore throat and a runny nose. It is good that we are returning to Lahore today. I can take her to the doctor in the evening."

Breakfast was eaten in silence. Asif did not comment on the thoughtfulness of procuring bread all the way from town but, at least, there were no adverse comments. By mid-morning the visitors were ready to depart. Kaneez Fatima brought forth an exquisitely embroidered *chadar* to gift to Shehla.

"This is the first time you have come to my house, *dulhan*, so here is a *chadar* for you."

"It is gorgeous, thank you. I love it. But what is it for?"

"It is a *chadar*," repeated Kaneez Fatima, puzzled, "When you go shopping you can cover yourself with it."

"Oh! Apa," Asif said, "Shehla doesn't need a *chadar* to go shopping. We are more modern than that!"

"But it is beautiful," said Shehla with an appeasing smile, "and I will use it as a table cloth. Thank you so much."

The visit of her brother left Kaneez Fatima in a daze. Nothing she did, or cooked or said had been met with approval. In fact she had been made to feel like a peasant.

And now here was her precious Munir going to stay with the same bizarre woman. Kaneez Fatima could envision poor Munir shivering all night under a flimsy blanket and then being made to drink tea without sugar and eat bland, oil less food laid out on embroidered *chadars*. Yet there was no alternative. To put Munir in the college boarding when his uncle lived in the same city would mean severing all connections with her brother forever.

In the event, only Kaneez Fatima remained unhappy and dissatisfied with the arrangement. Majid was thankful that he did not have to foot the bill of Munir's boarding and lodging from his increasingly meager monthly income. Other grocery stores had opened in the village which were better stocked and more in tune with customers' needs.

Munir was so happy to get to Lahore that the living arrangements did not make a difference to him. He had outgrown his school and his childhood companions a long time ago. That he was now attending Government College, Lahore, the elevated bastion of learning he had always dreamed about, was enough to counteract the inconvenience of blankets and sugarless teas.

In fact, after a few weeks of adjustment he actually started to like Shehla's way of housekeeping. He was treated like an adult by everyone. Even if his favorite foods were absent from the table, at least there was no one to remind him to brush his teeth before bedtime or to insist on massaging his head with oil to safeguard his brain power.

The servants called him Munir *sahib*. Rabab, his cousin who was two years younger, addressed him as Munir Bhai, and his uncle and aunt listened to his views and opinions whenever they had the time to spend with him. Mainly he was left to his own devices. He spent the biggest chunk of the day at college. He was dropped there by his uncle's driver in the morning and came home by bus when his classes were done. When he returned, a servant got him food and he ate it alone in the dining room. His aunt and cousin had lunch together when Rabab returned from school. He had company for lunch only if, by chance, he came home when the women of the household were eating. The family had the evening meal together when Asif and Shehla were not dining out. That is when Munir was encouraged to participate in grown up dinner conversation and to interact with his uncle and aunt.

Rabab, being an only child, was also often on her own. As time passed the youngsters found it was pleasant to spend time together. So whenever her homework was done and her daily phone chats with her friends were over, Rabab would knock on Munir's door. Munir would eagerly join her in front of the TV in the lounge. Rabab considered him, a college boy, the fount of all wisdom and Munir developed into a confident young man under the influence of this hero worship. They watched TV, listened to music, related anecdotes from college and school, sometimes even quarreled.

And so the years passed. When Munir was admitted to King Edward Medical College, Rabab completed Matric and joined Kinnaird College. They were both busier with their own lives now but always managed to find a little time to be together. Sometimes they just sat silently in the lounge, each reading a course book.

Munir spent every summer in the village. After his stint in the city even the first summer palled on him. But he was a dutiful young man and knew how much his mother missed him. During the summer, he read voraciously, went on long walks and smilingly ate whatever his mother cooked for him. Two months were not long and he soon returned to his real life.

Asif and family spent a month in Nathia Gali in the summer. They shared the ownership of a house there with a friend and the trip to the mountains had become an annual ritual. As the fourth summer of Munir's sojourn in Lahore rolled round, his uncle asked him whether he would like to go to Nathia Gali with them. Munir had not been invited before because Asif did not want to encroach on Kaneez Fatima's time with her son. But this year Asif was in the middle of finalizing a deal in Lahore. He would need to travel back and forth between Lahore and Nathia Gali in order to attend meetings in the city. If Munir were to go with them, Asif could leave his family under Munir's care with an easy mind.

Munir agreed with alacrity. He had not been looking forward to two dull months in the village. He immediately wrote to his mother that his arrival would be delayed and started packing. He had never been anywhere other than Lahore and the village and Nathia Gali sounded like heaven. He asked Rabab's advice about what would be needed and packed accordingly.

Munir enjoyed even the drive to Islamabad. They stopped for lunch at the house of Asif's friend in Islamabad and Munir drank in the sights and sounds of the Capital. As they resumed their journey and the corkscrew roads of the hills were broached, Munir's excitement infected Rabab who had previously considered the car trip to Nathia Gali rather tedious. And the journey set the tone for the entire stay at Nathia Gali. Rabab saw everything with Munir's eyes and was wonderstruck. His companionship made the most humdrum tasks fun. The month passed in a blur of laughter and happiness and Rabab returned to Lahore more or less in love with her cousin.

Shehla saw what was happening to her daughter and was content. In the years Munir had been living with them, she had found him to be all that she would want in a son-in-law.

Three more years passed and Munir graduated as a doctor. Rabab had completed BA the year before and was working with a women's magazine. Munir often made fun of the lax timings of her job and said it was just an excuse to dress up and leave home every day. She smiled at the teasing and did not take offence for now her cousin was very dear to her.

Many marriage proposals had been coming for Rabab as she was a pretty girl, well brought up, educated and from a well-to-do family. But Shehla had either declined or stalled the offers. She waited for Munir to complete his studies. Then one evening Shehla and Asif invited Munir to the drawing room and Shehla told him how much they liked him, how it was time for Rabab to get married and how they must take the proposals for her hand seriously and make the decision for her future. Asif added that they would consider no other proposal if one were to come from Kaneez Fatima. It was up to Munir.

Munir walked back to his room with his head in the clouds. He realized how far he had come from the village. As for Rabab marrying anyone else, he was appalled. He had never examined his feeling for his cousin, companion and friend. But he felt that his life would not be complete without her. Before he began the mandatory house job, he went to the village to speak to his mother.

On the day of his return his mother arranged a party for the entire village. Her son was now Dr. Munir. The next day at breakfast Munir broached the subject of proposing to Rabab and was horrified at the ugly scene that ensued. Kaneez Fatima was first dumb struck and then cursed Shehla roundly for stealing her son as payment for harboring him all these years. There was no way she would countenance this alliance. She was not good enough for Shehla but now the *harrafa* wanted Kaneez Fatima's son. Well, she would get him only over her dead body.

Stunned at the outburst, Munir tried to reassure his mother by telling her that he really loved Rabab and wanted to marry her and that Shehla Mumani was actually a nice person. Kaneez Fatima sat back holding her head in her hands.

"She has done black magic on you. Oh, I knew nothing good would come out of sending you to them. They have stolen my son from me."

She keened and wailed, beat her breast and whipped herself into a frenzy of hysteria. Nothing Majid or Munir could say changed her view.

Munir stayed for two more days to reason with his mother but she was adamant. It was a matter of choosing the uncle's family or her. And she was loud in reminding him that if he chose incorrectly she would not forgive him in this world or the next. Majid commiserated with his son but could do nothing to change his wife's views. Finally Munir left.

On his return, Munir told Asif about his mother's reaction. Then he packed and left to stay with a friend. After a few days he moved to a paying guest situation and completed the house job without ever visiting his uncle again. He busied himself to make arrangements for postgraduate studies in England and left for London the day he completed the house job. He did visit the village once before he left, to bid goodbye to his parents.

Rabab got married soon after Munir's departure from Lahore and so did he. Loneliness drove him into the arms of a sympathetic British nurse in the hospital where he worked and he married her within the year. She was a good woman and they made a comfortable life for themselves. He never visited Pakistan again, but wrote to his uncle regularly. Once a month he called his parents as long as they were alive and sent them ample funds to make their lives comfortable. But none of Kaneez Fatima's entreaties moved him to visit them or invite them to England. Broken bonds are often impossible to mend.

The story was riveting but I could see no way in which it impacted my life. Ammi didn't even have a brother and I harbored no secret love for anyone, cousin or otherwise. Ghazala's fiancé was a cousin but that was a happy engagement and no one was barring the way to matrimony.

Abba broke the silence. "What a great storyteller you are, Hassan! You should take up writing, you know, stories and such."

"Kamal Bhai, I do write. Some of my plays have even been broadcast on BBC radio."

Now that was a revelation. We all looked at Hassan Khalu with awe. Even Farida Khala was silenced; there was a writer in our midst! Hassan Khalu was bombarded with questions about how and when and what he wrote. He answered everyone patiently and seriously. The conversation turned away from my marriage prospects and I heaved a sigh of relief. But back in our room Ghazala and I nearly split our sides with laughter as we mimicked Farida Khala insulting us.

The aunts left for Multan after a few days and we returned to our regular routines. Zahid Bhai came over for dinner, as he did nearly every week, and I told him about my writer uncle. Zahid Bhai was more interested to know that Hassan Khalu lived in Manchester because he was expecting to do postgraduate work in that city. He told me he was getting close to his goal and could leave within months. That made me sad. But I smiled and told him that I was glad for him.

Later that week two sets of people came to 'see' me and they were as different from each other as night and day, literally. The first was a relative of Hassan Khalu. He was an engineer on the point of leaving for the U.S. to do his Masters. His family came in full force and formed a wall of coffee-colored faces for me to look at as I rolled in the tea trolley. Everyone had extremely dark complexions and even though no one in our family had unreasonable prejudices, six or eight dark brown people crowded in an average sized drawing room can be overwhelming. I didn't let my poise waver and went and sat in the chair strategically left vacant for me near the engineer. I found him to be well-spoken and pleasant to look at despite his color. The fifteen minutes we spent together went by quickly.

Two days later they called to say they would like their engineer son to marry me. My mother gave them the usual answer of 'we need time to decide,' but I overheard her tell my father that their skin color was casting a pall on her decision. My father told her not to be silly and that he expected more rational thought from her. I had found the engineer to be amiable enough but I decided not to let my mother's comment worry me. I did like some marriage prospects better than others but my heart was not engaged and I was carefree about the whole exercise. I relied on Ammi and Abba to find me the perfect spouse.

That very night one of my mother's friends came with a family of four at about dinner time. This friend of Ammi's, Nafees Auntie, had not called earlier to set up an appointment. She just walked in with the guests about ten minutes before we normally sat down for dinner. I was not wearing my Ammi- approved clothes and the tea trolley was not ready. Abba had already changed into pajamas after a hard day and was wearing his plaid dressing gown which was a little frayed at the collar and cuffs. Ammi pasted on her company smile, told me in an undertone to fix my hair and see to the trolley and sailed into the drawing room, closely followed by Abba. I hastily dragged a comb through my hair and went to tell the cook to ready the trolley with teacups, etc. while I rummaged in the freezer for my mother's cache of cakes and *samosas*. The cook began to fry the *samosas* and I cut up the cake into slices to hasten its thaw (Mrs. Bhimjee to the rescue!). Then I too went to see what Nafees Auntie had on offer.

This time the four faces that looked up as I entered were so white they nearly merged with our off white walls! I went in and sat in my designated chair but since I knew nothing about the gentleman by my side I had nothing to say. After a few minutes he began by asking me what I did. I replied and countered by asking him the same question. He, it turned out, was a pilot in the

Pakistan Air Force. The thought that he must look really dashing in uniform flashed into my mind. We both remained a little tongue tied and when I was sent to get the tea trolley I escaped with a sigh of relief. My job ended with bringing the trolley into the room because as I placed it near Ammi she gave me the sign to leave the room.

Nafees Auntie and company did not linger after tea and we sat down to dinner only one hour later than usual. Ammi was not amused by her friend's presumption, as she termed it. Such visits always followed a protocol. First a phone call was made to suggest a suitable match. Then Ammi asked a whole slew of questions about the young man like what his father did, what he did for a living, what his educational qualifications were, what his family background was and only after receiving satisfactory answers to all these questions was the family permitted to come to meet me. None of these steps were followed by Nafees Auntie and Ammi was annoyed.

"If only she had spoken to me earlier," Ammi said with a frown, "I would have told her we are not considering pilots. They aren't highly educated and if they are grounded because of ill health they have no way to earn a decent living. Besides they are liable to crash their plane and die young. But Nafees is never one to toe the line."

The same evening as we sat in front of the TV with Madam Noor Jehan holding forth in one of her glittering saris, the phone rang. Nafees Auntie was calling to announce that I had been approved by the pilot and his pale-skinned family. Ammi went into a long, diplomatic explanation of why she had to say no even though Nafees Auntie was recommending the family so highly. Abba dozed through the phone call and I read my book: Ammi could take care of it all.... as always.

CHAPTER 11

The month of December brought with it the promise of cool weather and college vacations. Kites had been rending the air for some weeks with their high pitched mating calls, and that, together with the ineffable winter smell in the mornings, heralded the coming of Karachi's best season. The skies were a lovely royal blue, the sunlight slanted in buttery yellow rays, humidity dropped and the temperature hovered around an ideal 70 F.

Ghazala confided that her fiancé, Sardar, was coming to Karachi for a visit. He would spend the bulk of his vacation from Cambridge University in Lahore but a week was allotted to Karachi. I was eager to meet Sardar. Besides, his visit would mean many interesting outings for all of us. All in all, December was shaping up well.

I wished Nadeem Bhai was also coming to Karachi in December. I missed him so much! But he was not in college and had no vacation as such. Besides he had left less than a year ago, so there were no plans afoot for a visit from him. As Ammi often reminded us, 'money didn't grow upon trees.' So I wrote long letters to him and got short replies in return. He was not much of a writer at the best of times and now he was busy coming to grips with his new profession.

He had chosen Chartered Accountancy himself, against our parents' advice of medicine as a career. He was good at numbers and literally cringed at the sight of blood so it did seem like a good choice. But I knew he had found it uphill work to get used to living in a small room in Liverpool, doing all his own chores and getting adjusted to life as an articled clerk.

At the beginning of the month Ammi entrusted me with hosting a dinner party. Abba had a circle of friends who met every week over dinner trying to lay to rest the problems of the world. Generally they met in the house of Mr. Khawar, an eminent lawyer. But once a year, when his cook was away on his month's leave, the venue became itinerant. On one of those four gypsy Tuesdays everyone came to our house for dinner and discussion.

Years of entertaining had taught Ammi that men were not into vegetables or dessert and that they liked indigenous dishes best. So her menus for Abba's friends concentrated on Pakistani meat dishes and ended with store bought dessert. Ammi did not believe in wasted effort.

This year the Tuesday on which we had to play host clashed with the birthday party of Ammi's friend. At first Ammi decided to forgo the birthday party because of Abba's pals, but when I assured her that I could manage on my own she agreed to leave the oldies to my mercies. The simple menu needed no last minute adjustments and garnishing from her and could be handled by the cook. Still, by the time Ammi left for her friend's, she had made sure that the food was cooked, the table laid and the cook briefed on exactly how to serve the meal. My job was simply to greet my 'uncles' and see that they were comfortable and that their plates were full throughout dinner.

All of Abba's friends loved the food and I saw to it that they ate more than enough of it. When they settled again in the drawing room, I served them brimming cups of hot tea. The evening was still young and the main business of discussion and dissent was about to begin. I decided to sit in for a while and hear what was holding the interest of Abba's group these days. So I settled in a corner in the spindly, uncomfortable chair which had been rejected by all the discerning guests.

After a few minutes of silence in which only loud slurping was heard from the assembled tea connoisseurs, Khawar Uncle cleared his throat.

"You know we have two sons, too young to get married of course, but I hope they find good wives and live happy lives."

"This is a new thought," said Imtiaz Uncle, who owned a string of petrol stations. "People worry about the marriages of their daughters but never of their sons. Sons make their own destiny."

"That is the received wisdom, I know," replied Khawar Uncle. "In the olden days it may have been so, but not now. Don't we all know of men whose lives have been blighted because of their wives?"

"Yes, yes," laughed Yunus Uncle who was also a doctor. "We all know of those hen-pecked weaklings who don't know how to manage their domestic affairs. But really, Khawar, the fault is their own."

"No, I don't agree." Khawar Uncle was adamant. "If you get tied to the wrong woman you can be miserable."

Now who should speak up but Haseeb Uncle, Abba's oldest friend; he and Abba had been neighbors when they were boys and each had grown up to be well known in his own field. Haseeb Uncle was a professor of Physics at Karachi University. He was normally a listener and let the others hold forth while he fiddled with his pipe.

"Actually Khawar is right," he said in his quiet way. "And I can tell you a story that would prove the point. The tale that I am going to relate happened in my wife's family and I saw it unfold with my own eyes right from the first day. So you can be sure of its veracity."

"Haseeb is going to tell a story!" Imtiaz Uncle announced. "All of you keep quiet and attend to him; it isn't often that Haseeb volunteers to speak at all. Yes, yes, Haseeb, we are all ears now."

Haseeb Uncle paused to refill his pipe and I got a fresh pot of tea. There was no way I was going to miss this story. I had heard enough tales of marital woes related by females. I needed to hear the male view of the matter too. After a few tentative puffs on the pipe, Haseeb Uncle looked around to ensure he had everyone's attention and then began.

THE STORY OF THE RECALCITRANT WIFE

Karim was born to Naseema after five stillbirths. She had made a *mannat* at *Data Sahib* that she would take the baby to the *dargah* within a week of the birth if she had a living healthy baby. Now Naseema was in a fix. She was deeply grateful that she finally had a live baby, and a boy at that, but she could not see herself taking him to the *dargah* within the week. The birth had been extremely painful, for after fifteen hours of labor the doctor had decided to do a C-section. Naseema was weak from loss of blood and in no condition to undertake the rigors of a visit to *Data Sahib*. Yet, she feared for the health and safety of the child if the *mannat* was not fulfilled. So she asked her older sister to carry the baby to the *dargah*.

Naseema's older sister, Roshan Ara, had always been averse to *mannats* and visits to the tombs of holy men. She felt that such practices were un-Islamic and bordered on the pagan. However, Naseema's agitation could not be ignored. Much against her own inclinations, Roshan Ara agreed to her sister's request.

Naseema told her sister to come and fetch the baby. Meanwhile, the baby was fed, bathed, perfumed and clad all in white. His eyes were lined with *surma*, and a black dot was placed on his forehead to ward off the evil eye. Rs. 101 in rupee coins were placed in a white cloth bag stitched expressly for this purpose. These would be presented to the *dargah* official to be distributed among the poor.

Roshan Ara found all the preparations distasteful but her love for her sister prevailed. She was driven to the *dargah* where she got off with the baby in her arms and walked barefoot, as the *mannat* required, to the tomb itself. The money was given to the caretaker and Roshan Ara hurried out. She wanted to leave the overcrowded area before the baby caught any germs from the coughing, spitting multitude heaving around her and also before the baby was assailed by hunger and started to wail.

Karim suffered no ill effects from the outing. As the years went by he grew to be a lusty young lad, taller than his contemporaries and somewhat muffin-faced. Naseema never conceived again and after her husband died of a cardiac infarction, all her hopes and ambitions centered on her son. For her he was better than the most handsome prince. She loved him unconditionally. "I am going to make him a doctor," she told all and sundry with great pride. And Karim seemed to absorb her expectations for he became diligent in his studies. He never disobeyed his elders and was a model child and adolescent, if a trifle stolid.

In time he completed MBBS and proceeded to England to work toward an MRCP. When he was preparing for the final exam, he heard that Nadia, his *mamun's* daughter, was about to get engaged. He immediately telephoned his mother; the first time since he had arrived in the UK. After some hemming and hawing, he divulged his great love for Nadia and his desire to marry her. Naseema was speechless. She had never liked the girl and thought her too flighty and modern. Moreover, now when the engagement party was only two weeks away how was she to present her son's case to her brother? Her brother was bound to ask why she had not spoken earlier. She could hardly tell him that she had never considered Nadia to be a suitable daughter-in-law. Yet now when her prince, her son, had declared his love, Naseema would go to any length to make sure that his wish was fulfilled.

After reassuring Karim that she would do her best, Naseema sat down to make plans. Once again she could think only of Roshan Ara as a likely ally. Once again Roshan Ara, found the job thrust upon her quite objectionable. Here was a girl promised to another and now at the last moment, Roshan Ara was to go and convince her brother that he should renege on his word to the prospective groom, break off the engagement and, instead, betroth the girl to Karim. Roshan Ara was worried both about the ethics of the situation and her brother's reaction and was unsure of Nadia's acquiescence to the scheme. The whole situation was fraught. Yet, once again, Roshan Ara could not withstand the entreaties of her sister to which, this time, the pleas of her nephew were also added.

For three days she camped in her brother's house. She refused to leave till he agreed to her proposal. He was not easy to convince and his repeated question of why Naseema had not asked for his daughter's hand earlier was unanswerable. All Roshan Ara could reiterate was that Karim loved Nadia and that his life would be ruined if he could not marry her. She portrayed Karim's devotion in glowing terms and painted vivid pictures of how forlorn and dejected he would be if Nadia was lost to him. She also touched upon the glory of being married to an MRCP and the wealthy lifestyle that

Nadia would have. Finally she reminded her brother of his fraternal duty to Naseema and that she, Naseema, had never asked him for anything before.

After two days of constant badgering, Roshan Ara convinced her brother of the superior claim of Karim to Nadia's hand. The sticking point was that he had already given his word to the other party, who were also distant cousins. At this point an unexpected voice joined Roshan Ara's. Nadia told her mother that she wanted to marry Karim. Since Nadia had previously shown a very obvious preference for the man she was about to be affianced to, her mother was puzzled at this change of heart.

What had happened was that Nadia, who was an avid reader of Mills and Boons romances, was quite swept away by Roshan Ara's descriptions of Karim's love for her. If serious, sober Karim was ready to flout convention, defy his elders and be brazen enough to lay bare his love for her in front of everyone, then he was the man for her. Her eyes grew misty at the thought of his anguish and devotion. She had to marry her passionate admirer and she told her mother that she would accept no one but Karim.

On the third day Roshan Ara won the approval of her brother. He might have been able to withstand his sister but he had no chance against his wife and daughter. Nadia's engagement was broken a week before the scheduled party and she was affianced to Karim posthaste. For the second time in Karim's life Roshan Ara had come to the rescue.

Because of the scandal of the broken engagement it was decided that Nadia and Karim's wedding should take place as soon as possible. Karim put away his books, postponed taking his exam and headed for home. Naseema, who had been envisioning Karim's wedding for years, went into a frenzy of preparation. The wedding was a gala event against which other family weddings were measured for years to come. Nadia became Karim's wife and so started his tale of woe.

Nadia was a pretty girl and made a stunning bride. But when she saw Karim rigged out in a *sherwani* and *saafa* her heart sank.

Always plain, he looked nearly comical in the unaccustomed attire. The romance of defying her parents to marry the suitor of her choice evaporated as Nadia gazed at her unsmiling and unlovely groom. In her zeal to marry her supposed hero she had forgotten how plain he'd always been. Now she remembered her discarded suitor with regret. His looks were nearly perfect.

And things did not become better in the days that followed. Karim never looked handsome no matter what he wore. He was of a serious disposition and not prone to laughter. He did nothing on the spur of the moment or against his family's wishes. His one defiance had been more than enough for him. He was now content with his life and was making plans for taking his bride to the UK and then sitting for the crucial exam.

Nadia was enjoying the importance that was accorded to her bridal status. She was also relishing getting adorned every evening in shimmering new clothes and jewelry and receiving compliments on her looks and even envious glances from her unmarried cousins. But that is where her happiness ended. She was aghast at her own fate and could not understand how or why she had allowed herself to be saddled with a pasty-faced and boring husband. She was the prettiest of all her contemporaries. She had a perfect figure and excellent taste in clothes. So why did she have to be burdened with this insipid man who never uttered endearments or whispered compliments in her ear? Sana, her cousin who was as plain as a bun, had a tall, dashing army captain for a husband. Yet she, Nadia, who had spurned a handsome fiancé, had Karim instead.

When the time came to accompany Karim to England, she flatly refused. She did not want to leave her family and friends and go where she would have to cook and clean and cater to the comfort of her lump of a husband. No way was she going to play servant to tongue tied, insignificant Karim!

So Karim went to the UK alone and called her every day during his study breaks. She was not always available to take his calls and had no time for long chats. When he sat for and failed the exam, Nadia was livid. She did not know how to face the world. At least if he had become a hot shot doctor and lavished his money on her she could have tolerated his appearance. But now it seemed her husband was deficient both in looks and lucre. She wondered what she had done to deserve such a nincompoop.

Without hesitation she passed on her feelings of being short-changed to Karim. And Karim, who was already dejected, never having failed an exam before, was devastated by Nadia's condemnation. Alone and depressed as he was in the bleak climate of England, he yearned in vain for a word of encouragement or fondness from his wife. Instead, all his failings, even his receding hairline, were disdainfully enumerated by Nadia on the rare occasions that she deigned to speak to him on the phone. Slowly poor Karim came to believe that he really was a loser. He began to view himself as incompetent and unlovable and so he failed at the next two attempts at the exam also.

During all this time Nadia stayed in Karachi and only jeered at his incompetence on the phone. She categorically refused to join him in England. She had no desire to sacrifice her comfort for a husband who had fallen so short of her expectations. Naseema felt that Nadia's ministrations would make Karim's life more comfortable and her encouragement would help him study better. Nadia replied that she was not a nursemaid and that it was the duty of husbands to look after wives, not the other way round. She taunted Karim that he was not earning anything and she had to be beholden to his mother for her expenses.

"What sort of husband are you, Karim? Have you done one single thing that you should be doing? Here I am, bored and imprisoned in your mother's house. I have no money for shopping and no parties to go to. And you can't even pass a simple exam. What am I getting out of this marriage?"

Karim could have asked Nadia the same question. His wife was beating down his spirit, massacring his self-esteem and making him aware of every one of his flaws. After he failed the third time and digested all that Nadia had to say, he came to the conclusion that his sanity was in jeopardy. His feelings for Nadia had died a long time ago and now his marriage expired too. From some nearly forgotten instinct of self-preservation he drew the strength to call Naseema and tell her to begin divorce proceedings.

This time Roshan Ara refused to help her sister point blank. She knew that Nadia had her faults and even that she may have been the prime cause of the break up, but she did not want to take the part of one sibling against the other. So Roshan Ara remained studiously aloof from the whole drama. Naseema and her lawyer did Karim's bidding.

The divorce went through. Karim was bad-mouthed among the entire family, first for breaking Nadia's engagement and then ending the marriage. It was entirely his fault. In all such cases the man is always the culprit. No one wants to know the whole story. The female is the one who has to bear the stigma of divorce so she is presumed to be the victim.

Naseema and her brother broke off relations with each other. At this point Roshan Ara did mediate and try to bring them to an understanding. She did not want them to arrive at point non plus because of their children. But neither came round to her point of view. They even stopped acknowledging each other if they happened to attend the same family function and Naseema did not attend her brother's funeral when he died a couple of years later. Mercifully Nadia had remarried in his lifetime, to the very suitor who was rejected earlier, and seemed to be well enough in her careless and peevish way.

Poor Karim took a longer time to recover from his ordeal. His career was at a standstill and remarriage did not even figure in his plans. His confidence had been shaken and his world view had undergone a metamorphosis. Never had he failed at anything in his life before the cataclysmic event that was his marriage. And then he failed so monumentally that all his previous notions about his abilities and about love were shattered. He might have been able to cope with one letdown at a time but the double whammy of enduring the scorn of his bride and his own repeated failure to pass the MRCP exam sent him spiraling into depression.

He returned to Pakistan as soon as the divorce was finalized and went into hibernation. He took to his bed and could bear the company only of his mother. Naseema's heart hardened against her brother and Nadia when she saw what agony her beloved son was going through and what her prince had been reduced to. No wonder she snapped at Roshan Ara when reconciliation was broached. In turn, Roshan Ara realized the hopelessness of her mission when she saw Karim, diminished and dispirited.

After a year and a half of licking his wounds, Karim could finally be made to talk of his future. Naseema made him see that hiding from the world was no remedy for his misfortunes. She talked about the U.S. as an alternative to the UK. She gave him examples of those of his friends who were doing well there. Gradually Karim got tired of inactivity and became more inclined to bestir himself. He started preparing for the ECFMG exam and a year later when he passed it with flying colors his confidence surged back. Naseema continued to buoy Karim's spirits but on the sly she also started looking for a wife for him. It was not in her plans to send him alone to far-off America.

By the time Karim was ready to apply for medical residencies in the U.S., Naseema had a first-class candidate lined up for him. But when she introduced the subject of marriage to Karim, he reacted violently. "Never again," he stated vehemently. He was never going to lay himself open to heartbreak and ridicule from such an intimate source.

For the third time in Karim's life Roshan Ara came to the rescue. This time Naseema did not need to convince her to help. Roshan Ara had come to the conclusion herself that enough was enough. Karim had been wallowing in depression and self-pity for years and now needed to return to the land of the living. She button-holed Karim in his room and spent the better part of the day with him till finally he smiled and nodded at her suggestions.

The girl identified by Naseema, Asma by name, was stunning to look at but quiet, gentle and self effacing. No one had set her up as the beauty of the family. Moreover, she had gone through an even worse experience than Karim had. Married off at eighteen to the highly educated son of an industrialist, she discovered that her husband was a sadist by nature. The more she bore his abuse silently the worse his treatment became. At first she did not say anything to her family but when she ended up in the hospital, a month after the wedding, with multiple fractures and a face so bruised and swollen that not even her mother was sure of her identity, the truth came out. She never returned to her husband and the marriage ended.

Asma had been the shy, retiring type to begin with and her marital experience had drained her life of all joy. When Naseema began to notice her, she was only twenty-one years of age and was slowly responding to the loving ministration of her family. Naseema was a close friend of a neighbor of Asma's parents and so was cognizant of all the facts of Asma's marriage. She had even met Asma at her friend's house a few times. To Naseema, Asma was the ideal wife for her Karim: Decorative but not flamboyant, and with a past that was sure to touch Karim's soft heart. In trying to make Asma happy, Naseema was sure he would put aside his own misgivings about relationships.

Naseema's prediction proved to be correct. She knew her son. When she next broached marriage to Karim, she also presented the case of Asma to him.

"You will become her supporter and protector and she will be your helpmate in everything." Naseema explained. "Being in America will be good for her too. How long can she listen to people gossiping about her here? Take her and make a new life for yourself and for her in the U.S."

Once Karim saw the wisdom of his mother's advice everything fell into place. He was accepted to a residency program in Iowa, meetings were arranged between him and Asma, mutual liking led to a marriage proposal, and within two months the two were married and on their way to the new world! This time the bride did not have any reservations about his looks. He was still as plain as before but Asma saw only the kindness in his eyes. As for Karim the worshipful looks he got from Asma were enough to set him up for life and make him vow to cherish this gift from heaven who was his bride. Because of their respect for each other, perhaps also because of the pain and disillusionment of their previous experiences, the marriage flourished.

In a few years Karim set up his private practice and began to rake in the dollars. Asma continued to idolize her husband as she presided over the house, cared for her children and welcomed Naseema into the family when the older lady migrated to live with them.

So you see a good marriage is as essential for a man as for a woman. People often pray for the happiness of their daughters knowing a bad marriage for a female is enough to ruin her life. Almost no one prays for a happy marriage for sons. It is believed that males can just walk away unscathed from disastrous marriages. But it is not so. Men have hearts too and their egos are fragile enough to be shattered and mutilated.

⸻⸻◈⸻⸻

As the story wound down and Haseeb Uncle stuck his pipe back into his mouth, I was elated. It was empowering to know that women could influence the flow of life for both good and bad.

"That is only one case," said Yunus Uncle, still unconvinced, "and our hero seems to have been spineless."

Abba smiled and said, "I think you are being a little harsh, Yunus. Being sensitive is not the same as being weak. And we all know how much we owe to our wives. If they had not been there to support us through the bad times I don't know how many of us would have turned out to be successful."

"Hear, hear," Khawar Uncle said. "Thank you, Haseeb, for making my point for me. I hope my sons get wives who complement them and that there is mutual respect between the spouses."

"Speaking of respect," Yunus Uncle pointedly changed the topic, "I can have no respect for our holy President."

Now that politics became the theme of discussion, I decided that my room afforded better entertainment.

I joined the uncles when the time came for them to depart. I smiled and said *Khuda Hafiz* and made sure they remembered to take all their belongings with them. Just then Ammi returned and approved of my gracious hostess role.

Ghazala became very busy in the ensuing weeks as Ainee Auntie was getting a new wardrobe for her to wear during Sardar's visit. She became even busier when Sardar reached Karachi. I was invited to lunch one day to meet him and to play some sort of a chaperone, since we three would be on our own at the Chinese restaurant. Sardar had chosen the restaurant because he missed the Pakistani style of Chinese food in England.

I found Sardar to be quite worthy of Ghazala, which was high praise in my book. He wasn't very handsome but had a pleasant face and a ready smile. He kept us in whoops during lunch as he related one joke after another but was just as ready to hear and laugh at any funny anecdotes we narrated. I found his best qualities to be the gleam of appreciation in his eyes when he looked at Ghazala and the consideration he showed to her wishes. After lunch we drove to Hill Park and I sat on a bench, with the excuse that my shoes were pinching me, and let the two wander around the winding paths on their own.

The next time I met Ghazala and Sardar was at the beach. A cousin of Ainee Auntie owned a luxurious villa on the beach at Hawke's Bay. This gentleman was in the construction business and, according to Ghazala, made use of the beach 'hut' by lending it to key bureaucrats with whom he wished to curry favor. Ainee Auntie had booked the hut weeks in advance of Sardar's arrival. Now her entire family congregated there, together with me, at Ghazala's invitation, and Karachi's best known caterer who was managing the all-important business of food.

Ammi reminded me to wear dark, thick clothes. I wasn't planning to go into the water much, surrounded as I would be with relative strangers, but a bit of wading was a must. And if in the process

I got drenched by a wayward wave my thick clothes would save me from becoming an Indian film heroine in the rain...nearly nude. Most of the other females had taken similar precautions with their clothes.

We got to Hawke's Bay at 11:30 a.m., after an hour's drive. A quick snack of coffee, cake, sandwiches and fruit was the first order of business and then the younger lot headed toward the sea. The men changed into swimming trunks and the women and girls tied their *dupattas* sash fashion across their bodies. The water was limpid and cool and so blue that it looked unreal. None of the females ventured beyond knee-high water except for the daughters of Ghazala's uncle who walked right in till all we could see were their heads. Better them than me, I thought. Karachi beaches were tricky places, though less so in winter, and I had been taught to respect the sea from an early age. Thankfully, all remained peaceful except for a false alarm spread by Ghazala's rascally young cousin that there were bluebottle jellyfish in the water.

All in all it was a memorable picnic and the food was divine. Spending more time with Sardar made me even happier for Ghazala. The week of his visit passed all too soon, but left us with the memories of innumerable events and many conversations to dissect and discuss during our winter break. I hoped that whoever was finally selected for me would give me as much pleasure in his company as Ghazala found in Sardar's.

CHAPTER 12

About a week after college resumed, Azra Khala called to say they were planning a big bash for Akbar's *Ameen*. At twelve years of age, Akbar, Azra khala's son, had completed the reading of the Holy Quran in Arabic. This usually called for a celebration. In the same situation, Ammi had just ordered a dessert of my choice. A generation or two ago, however, a party for the entire family used to mark the occasion. Azra Khala decided that she wanted to have a gala event, for family, friends and clients, and was going to make the *Ameen* a reason to do so.

The party would be held in the garden of her house. The weather was perfect and Azra Khala was sure to make it a grand affair. I told Ammi I wanted a new *jora* for the event. I had worn my *Eid joras* too many times already. My mother agreed, leaving me speechless and wary. I never got new clothes during the year and even though I had made my request I had no anticipation of its acceptance. Was Ammi well?

Seeing my bewilderment Ammi smiled and said, "We can have the fabric that Nusrat gave you stitched in time. It is a lovely shade of red and will look good on you."

"Oh! Goody," I said and gave her a hug. "I was afraid it was destined for the cold storage."

"No, not this time. I have plenty of fabric saved for your trousseau. Besides I want you to be well dressed when you go to parties. That is good exposure for you."

Finally something useful was coming out of this getting settled business. Who knew? I may even be allowed lipstick!

On the day of the *Ameen*, Ammi and I went to help Azra Khala right after breakfast. The professional cooks had already arrived and the food was being cooked in the small backyard. Unfortunately, it was of the humdrum *biryani, qorma, kheer* variety. But that is where the commonplace ended. The front garden was going to be a bower of blooms under a white *shamiana* which was even then being hauled up. The flower-beds were full of petunias which Azra Khala's gardener had planted early so that they were a riot of red. The plan was to have garlands of fragrant white *motia* and red roses looped in all the trees and on the trellises and covering the inside surfaces of the boundary walls. All the rented furniture and crockery were also red and white. A small elevated area, a stage for the ceremony, had a red backdrop and a grand white sofa with red throw pillows for Akbar to sit on. It was going to be flanked with arrangements of red and white flowers.

The whole décor was wasted on Akbar and his brother, Aslam. They were still at the stage when bathroom jokes and spitballs made their day. Najeeb Khalu was out of his depth and so decided to keep to his room and Taimur, his eldest son, was not even present, having been posted to some godforsaken place as a lieutenant in the army. But Baji was having the time of her life as she supervised the cooks at the back. All the ingredients they needed had been bought beforehand and were secured by Baji. Now she was in charge of handing them to the cooks as the need arose. Whenever she had a free moment she would waddle to the front garden to feast her eyes on the arrangements.

When the three of us entered Azra Khala's garden that evening, we gasped with amazement. What we had appreciated in the glare of the sun was looking positively other worldly under the twinkling fairy lights and strategically placed spot lights. No wonder Azra Khala did so well at her interior decoration business! Najeeb Khalu and the two boys were dressed in white *sherwanis* and Azra Khala was wearing something loose and flowing in bright red. Baji bustled around in her habitual white and so everyone was color coordinated.

Around 8:00 p.m., when most of the guests had arrived, Akbar went to sit upon the sofa on the stage. Najeeb Khalu's eldest brother joined him there and the ceremony started. It was a simple one. As people gathered round the stage and fell silent, Akbar's uncle announced with pride that Akbar had completed the reading of the Quran. Then Akbar recited some verses from the Quran and everybody praised the fluency of his recitation. No clapping, of course. As soon as the uncle left the stage, people went up to congratulate Akbar and give him envelopes of cash. Azra Khala gestured to Ammi who went up and sat with him while Azra Khala left to order the dinner to be served.

I had seen some guests carrying in presents for Akbar. They must have been Azra Khala's clients. Traditionally cash was given at such events and no one in the know would have done anything different. After the party Azra Khala would make a list of names and amounts of the cash gifts so that she could give a little more than she received to each of the family members when they had similar celebrations. Nani had told me that often the cash gifts added up to what the host had spent on the party. The festivities did not become a financial burden. I grinned as I realized that Akbar was going to get very little of what he was hauling in.

All in all it was a lovely evening. I felt elegant in my rose red outfit and Ammi was proved right; I was accosted by two auntie types whom I didn't know. They asked me how I was related to Azra Khala. My inkling was that they were looking for a wife for some young man and I had caught their fancy. Sure enough a few days later I was told by Ammi that some people were coming to 'see' me in the next few days, courtesy of Azra Khala. Ho hum, the same merry-go-round again! I was getting sick of being exhibited over and over again. But the alternative, in which no one was interested in me at all, would have been worse.

The first group to arrive within a few days of the *Ameen* party was escorted by Azra Khala's, neighbor, Tanya Auntie. This lady lived right next door to Azra Khala and had become her close friend. Tall and raw-boned she was plain in face and plainer in dress. Her husband was a lawyer who had never done well financially. Early on in the marriage it had dawned upon her that she would have to supplement his income if she wanted luxuries. So she put her Master's degree to use and started teaching at a college. She used to say that her husband was a good man and a charming companion with only one fault: He was not a good provider. By taking up a job she made up for the drawback.

They had three daughters, the oldest about fifteen, all of whom, Ammi felt, Tanya Auntie was spoiling by over-indulgence. That left even less money for Tanya Auntie who scrimped on herself and dressed in below par clothes. "But nothing looks good on me," Tanya Auntie used to say with a laugh. "So why spend money on myself?"

Tanya Auntie brought her nephew, a doctor, together with his parents and sisters to our house. In my regulation pink clothes I entered with the tea trolley and went to sit by the candidate. When I looked up I realized I had met him before. Only a few weeks ago when Ainee Auntie had taken us to a film we had met Zahid Bhai and a friend of his at the cinema house. This guy was the friend. He recognized me too and we broke into speech simultaneously. All the awkwardness vanished in the subsequent laughter as we discussed the film we had seen. The fifteen minutes that were allowed by Ammi raced past and I left with a smile on my face.

The guests departed soon after but Tanya Auntie stayed back to plug her sister's family. My parents listened to the praises for a bit and then Ammi cut in. "Tanya, we don't know yet whether your sister and her son even liked Amna. I am sure they are nice people but we don't need to discuss them when there is no proposal on the table."

"The proposal is sure to come." Tanya Auntie looked at me with a grin. "Who can resist this gorgeous girl?"

"Many. Amna is no beauty," Ammi replied drily. Abba caught my eye and shook his head. I smiled back.

Tanya Auntie was not to be hushed. "Beauties are too highly rated. Very few beauties have achieved happiness. Cleopatra lost her kingdom and then got bitten by a snake, Marie Antoinette got her head chopped off, Princess Margaret was not allowed to marry her love and had to settle for a photographer and Jackie Kennedy first got married to a womanizer and then a caricature. No happiness. Even among normal, everyday people like us beauty attracts disasters. All my friends who are happy are plain or at most, slightly attractive. Beauty is a curse."

"Well, that is quite damning." Ammi laughed. "And such a comforting thought for all of us who are plain." She was being self-deprecating, for my mother was very pretty.

"You think I am joking? No, no, Rabia, I am very serious. I am so glad none of my daughters are beautiful. They are all pleasant looking and with correct grooming can be attractive. That's good. If they had real beauty I would be worried. I could tell you a dozen stories of girls whose beauty was legendary and who ended up unhappy. Actually, one such was my dear friend. Have I ever mentioned Samina to you?"

Ammi shook her head.

"Well then, what better time than now? Let's have another cup of tea and I will relate her history."

I went to the trolley to make a cup of tea and thought, oh no, not another beauty in distress story. It seemed that in the game of marriage, happiness was chancy at best but beauties were more often unlucky than not. My favorite novels had got it all wrong!

Tanya Auntie helped herself to Ammi's famed black forest cake and said, "Actually, my friend was a victim of circumstances. The world conspired against her and the conditions surrounding her turned her life into such a knotty problem that her beauty was unable to contend with it..."

The Story of the Beautiful Bengali

It amazes me to remember that I was married, a mother of two, and a college lecturer, and still so thoughtless in those days.

I should have been more aware. I have no idea why but I just went with the flow and never stopped to think or ask questions.

Things were bad in East Pakistan. But we in Karachi gave no thought to what was happening. We had always been oblivious to events in the east, even in the past. The hand-me-down belief about Bengalis not being as good as us had been swallowed whole. We sniggered about them being short and dark—even though many of us were shorter and darker. We also imagined they were lazy. There was a story about the rickshaw puller who only worked half the day to earn enough to buy food for his family for that day. He became the epitome of Bengali apathy. Why didn't he work the whole day and earn more than just his daily bread? Why did he not save the extra money and use it to better himself? Why was he content with so little and why so ready to sleep under the tree for the rest of the day? No West Pakistani would be so shortsighted. The rickshaw puller's story was repeated ad nauseam whenever the topic arose. Nobody asked if it was true.

Yet we all had Bengali friends in Karachi and somehow the taint of short, dark and lazy never stuck to them. We often forgot they were Bengali. My friend, Samina, was one of them. She had been with me throughout school and we were good friends. She was of average height and truly beautiful, a redhead with a milky white skin tone. She topped in every class throughout our entire school career and was an outstanding athelete. Her father was some big shot in the government who arranged our school trips to the Mint and Sind Assembly. Her mother was a talented cook and seamstress so the food served at Samina's house surpassed any we had elsewhere, and her clothes, when she was out of school uniform, were works of art.

We attended the same college and graduated together and then went on to do our Masters. I got married and settled down. She finished her studies and joined a multinational company. After a few years her father was transferred to East Pakistan. Her younger siblings despaired at having to live in Dhaka after a lifetime in Karachi. Samina understood their angst but kept her thoughts to herself and helped her family to pack, comforted her brother and sister and got herself transferred to Dhaka. Back in their hometown, the family pressure was such that only after a few months I received an invitation for Samina's wedding. About three months after that Samina was back in Karachi, after another company transfer, alone and divorced.

The husband had been so overwhelmed by the acquisition of a young, beautiful, talented bride who was also the daughter of a top government official that he could not quite believe his luck. He felt there had to be something wrong with her, some secret failing, by reason of which she had been palmed off on him. On the wedding night he made her take off all her clothes to examine her for physical defects. Then a doctor was called in to give her an internal examination to assure her virginity. Samina felt violated but bore all. The idea of walking out of her new 'home' and returning to her parents that very night, though attractive, was too demeaning to herself and her family.

The marriage that began so inappropriately continued down the same path and made both the protagonists more miserable by the hour. A month later Samina, unable to continue, went back to her parents and sued for divorce.

Back in Karachi it was not easy to pick up the threads of her life where she had left them only a few months back. People whispered about her. Bengalis in general were condemned as narrow-minded monsters because of how her husband had treated her. In the office her divorced status made her stand out like a sore thumb. So Samina applied for a scholarship to the U.S., won it easily and set off for the west.

During the years that she was away the disaffection in East Pakistan became bitter. It was only in retrospect that I realized the discontent and anger had always been there under the surface. Even in the 1950s, my uncle, who was posted for a few years in Chittagong while working for a government ministry, had received death threats. The threats were not against him personally but against a West Pakistani holding that office. He was mild-mannered and just and so he finally won the hearts of his subordinates. But the rest of the brash young West Pakistanis continued to exacerbate the situation and increase the hatred in Bengali bosoms.

The final straw came when the only fair elections Pakistan had ever seen brought forward Sheikh Mujibur Rehman as the winner. It was not only Bhutto, the runner up, who ranted that the reins of government should not be handed over to a Bingo. Most of us, including me, were swept away by the rhetoric and insisted that we did not want Bengalis as our rulers.

When I think back and try to figure out what my thought process was at that time, I find that I had none. I just mouthed what was the received opinion without a shred of conscious thought. Pakistan had had Bengali Prime Ministers in the past. No harm had been wrought by them. Moreover they were also Pakistanis. Why not have them rule us when we accepted Punjabis and Sindhis and Pathans? And why not remember that the curse of Martial Law had been imposed upon us by a non-Bengali and the one who was now most vocal against the dictates of the election results was also a non-Bengali?

We did not want to address the reason for Bengali anger at West Pakistan. We just wanted to condemn them out of hand and sweep them aside as complainers par excellence. We asked why they hated us so much, but it was just a rhetorical question. The reality that we looked down on them, made fun of them for being constantly hit by floods and cyclones, and felt, patently incorrectly, that they were a burden on the Pakistani economy, was never discussed.

When the explosion came we were left askance. We knew nothing but what the state-run TV and radio had been telling us. The tales told about the Mukhti Bahini and the Bengali separatists made us hate them. We all became champions of the Pakistan armed forces. The name of General Tiger Niazi resounded in every drawing room. Then suddenly the announcement was made that our valiant forces had laid down their arms. This was beyond our comprehension. The only way we could deal with the sense of betrayal and bewilderment was to see the breakup of our country as a good thing. We told each other that what had happened was going to be beneficial for Pakistan. There was a feeling of good riddance: If they want to be independent let them become independent, at least we will not have to foot the bill for their flood and cyclone relief.

It was Samina and families like hers that paid the price.

When the civil war started she wanted to hasten home from the U.S. but her father told her to complete her degree. Meanwhile, her father was put into a concentration camp with other Bengalis who did not want to see Pakistan truncated. At first they were labeled dangerous, then traitors. All their property was appropriated by the State. Samina's mother and younger brother and sister had to move in with an uncle, destitute.

Samina completed her degree a few months later and, not having a home in Dhaka, returned to Karachi where her father owned a house. She planned to live on the rental income while she looked for a job. But politics is a strange game. The house was confiscated by the Pakistani government since it belonged to a Bengali in Bangladesh. And so Samina ended up with us. Feelings were so high against the erstwhile East Pakistanis that I had to stop all visitors at the front door and alert them to the presence of a Bengali inside. Still the air often became electric with suppressed feelings and occasional eruptions of anger.

Samina's former employers rehired her and after a few months she moved into a guest house. It must have been a very difficult year for her. Her family was in a state of collapse in Dhaka and she had to face mental abuse of some sort on a daily basis in Karachi. Everyone was on edge.

After the ignominy of the surrender in Dhaka we were dealing with more than 90,000 of our people in Indian POW camps. 'Bengali' had become a curse word. The tension really came home to us one day when we found our cook beaten and bloodied in the kitchen. We had hired a part-time cook, a Bengali who was waiting to be repatriated, and he had proved to be a gifted chef and a good employee. That morning he was late. His clothes were torn and bloody. When asked for an explanation he broke down. For some reason he had

had to speak in the bus in which he was travelling. His accent identified him as a Bengali and that was enough for the passengers to gang up on him.

Finally Samina's father was released from the concentration camp and his brother set the family up in a rented house. Samina once again got herself transferred to Dhaka. At this time her earnings were crucial for the survival of the family. She paid for the marriage of her younger sister and sent her brother off to university in the UK on a scholarship.

Now for the crux of the story: A Scandinavian by the name of Berthold, Bertie as he was called by his friends, was a well-known journalist in Dhaka in those days. How Samina became acquainted with him was of no consequence, but meet him she did and promptly fell in love. He was older than her by more than a dozen years and twice divorced. But love is blind, as we know. After six months she approached her father about marrying him. Bertie was willing to convert, whatever that meant to an atheist, and so the marriage would be legal.

Samina's father had lost his country, his job, his properties and his standing in society. He lived on his brother's charity and the money that his daughter earned. He was not ready to lose even his dignity and see his daughter marry a foreigner. He utterly forbade the marriage. "Not while I am alive," he said.

Samina had thought that her family would take delight in her happiness and would share her joy in having found a soul mate at last. However, she was not willing to gratify her desires at the expense of her father's love. She dropped the idea of marriage, but her chaste friendship/love affair with Bertie continued. Bertie quite enjoyed this non-committal relationship and prolonged his sojourn even after Bangladesh stopped being in the news.

On Bangladesh's third birthday Samina's father died of a sudden heart attack. Even as his funeral rites were under way Samina could think of nothing but Bertie and her own loudly ticking biological clock. To make a long story short Samina married Bertie two months after her father's death. Bertie had been relocated to Melbourne by then and that is where Samina went after marriage.

The honeymoon period lasted six months and it was a time of unadulterated happiness for Samina. She played at being a housewife, learned to cook Scandinavian dishes and entertained Bertie's friends to many a smorgasbord to please him. Unfortunately her happiness was not to be a lasting one.

After Samina had mastered the arts of cleaning and cooking she wanted to graduate to the next level...motherhood. But Bertie had grown children from earlier marriages and did not want such a drastic addition to his life at his age. Since Samina could have no children without him she cajoled, persuaded, bickered, nagged and tried every other womanly wile to get her way, but to no avail. The marriage became a mockery. They loved each other still but this running battle spread a cancer through their relationship. All she wanted was the classic husband-babies marriage. Bertie, on the other hand, was happy to have a beautiful and loving wife but he did not want any alterations in his lifestyle. They managed to drag out their marriage for a while but finally the cracks became crevasses and when Bertie was transferred to South Africa, Samina returned to Dhaka.

Samina found a job again but not one as good as before. Moreover, she was now an estranged wife and more to be reviled than pitied. Only her mother was grateful to have her back as she was ailing and had no one else to look after her. Mercifully, Samina did not have to endure the slanderous tongues of her family for long, for her life soon took a new turn. Bertie called to tell her that he had been diagnosed with cancer and was dying.

Samina flew out to be with him at once. For the next ten months she nursed him day and night. Strangely the months were happy in many ways. They loved one another and there was no strife in the relationship anymore, only the shadow of death. The end was peaceful. Samina took the body to Sweden, interred him properly and returned to Dhaka.

Who could have guessed that Bertie's death would turn out to be a boon for Samina? First of all, as a widow she became respectable again. Secondly, she inherited a tidy sum from Bertie's estate and was assured of a pension for life from the Swedish government as Bertie's widow. She bought a house in a desirable locality of Dhaka, moved her mother there and hired a maid to look after her. For the first time in years she was able to live in her native land in the style that she had been used to while growing up in undivided Pakistan. Her life experiences helped her to begin writing a weekly agony-aunt column in a local newspaper and she gained fame and recognition.

Always beautiful she was now arrestingly so. But after two questionable forays into matrimony she chose to remain single. Her dream of a conventional life with husband and children was going to remain a dream forever.

———⸧«⬥»⸦———

Tanya Auntie dabbed her eyes as she trailed off. "We still write to one another and she is not unhappy, but very lonely. Once she loses her mother it will be worse. Her beauty has been of no use to her."

"What a sad story!" commented Abba, and then after a pause he chuckled and continued. "My mother was all for looks. She used to say that daughters-in-law must be good looking and good tempered and since one can't gauge tempers in drawing room meetings they certainly had to be pretty. Otherwise you could end up with neither one quality nor the other."

As Tanya Auntie opened her mouth to counter my father's remark, Ammi jumped in with, "He is just joking, Tanya. He knows that beauty is no guarantee for happiness."

I was enjoying the give and take without a shred of worry. This story could not be even vaguely directed at me, except in a positive way, for Ammi never tired of drumming into me that I was not beautiful. But Tanya Auntie's story made me cast my mind back eight or nine years when East Pakistan was becoming Bangladesh. I remembered serious discussions between my parents and their friends but only because such discussions meant that Nadeem Bhai and I were banished from the drawing room. That was all. Nothing that happened over there had had any effect on my daily life.

After Tanya Auntie left, I devoured the black forest cake to my heart's content and then snuggled against Abba to watch TV. The play 'Waris' was on. Abba kissed me on the top of my head and whispered, "You *are* beautiful." I gave him a beatific smile and all was right with the world.

The next week Azra Khala's Baji called to make an appointment for some relative of hers. The son was a banker in the new, dynamic, Pakistani bank, BCCI, and posted in Rome. The locale sounded good to my ears but by now I knew that reality rarely matched its advertisement.

As it happened, Zahid Bhai came to visit us almost at the same time as Baji and the banker's family walked in. When I trundled in the tea trolley I could see that he was sitting in the chair reserved for me and was looking visibly ill at ease. Ammi took control of the situation by telling Zahid Bhai to move by the banker's older brother and then gesturing at me to take the vacated seat. I felt shy with Zahid Bhai in the room. I always told him about the various people who came to 'see' me but having to deal with a prospect while Zahid Bhai was watching was awkward.

The banker had no such hang-ups. He started by asking me the obvious questions and soon put me at my ease. He must have been in the bank's customer relations department because he was a smooth talker. I quite enjoyed my fifteen minutes with him. Unfortunately, he was short, rotund and balding. But I knew Ammi would wave aside any comments on looks. What mattered was whether he was a nice person, she would say. But my grandmother's belief that if you were not careful you could end up with an ugly as well as a bad-tempered mate resounded in my ears. Oh, my!

When Baji and the banker's family left I re-entered the drawing room and asked Zahid Bhai to join me in polishing off the eats. Ammi's cooking restored the equilibrium and before long Zahid Bhai was his normal self. We had both recently seen the film 'Heaven

Can Wait' and I asked him how he liked it. He was going to be boring, I could see, and say it was entirely implausible.

"I know, I know," I said before he could speak. "It is only fantasy, but did you enjoy it?"

"Yes, but against my better medical judgment."

Then I related the coincidence of his friend from the movies coming to 'see' me and how funny it was that we both recognized each other at the same time. Zahid Bhai's face suddenly stilled. Without quite understanding his reaction I thought it best to change the topic of conversation.

The next day the families of both the doctor and the banker sent in their approval and Ammi answered with her now well known "We will need a little time to decide." I don't know how many enquiries she had instituted by now and how she was keeping everything straight. It was not my problem. In fact I had no problem at all apart from finishing my Psychology assignment on time.

CHAPTER 13

It was February and the cold weather was almost over. We were busy with parties and weddings as people crammed their various festivities in these last cool days before the grip of Karachi's long, sultry summer. And of course, there were 'viewing sessions' from time to time. I had decided not to get bugged by them. Instead, I was going to relax and enjoy myself. After all the guy was also under inspection so why should I alone feel like the victim?

The party I was eagerly awaiting was Ghazala's grandmother's 85th birthday which was going to be celebrated in Ghazala's house. It promised to be a grand affair. All of their relatives were congregating for the occasion. Most lived in Karachi but some of Ainee Auntie's siblings and cousins were coming from Lahore and Islamabad. My parents were invited to the party but I was to stay the entire weekend with Ghazala. It was going to be glorious!

It was a madhouse over there. Each room was occupied by entire families. Even Ghazala's room had sprouted an extra bed and two mattresses, all made up on the floor, meaning we would have two extra roommates. I was pushing my bag under one bed when in walked the pair who was going to share the room with us. Ghazala introduced us.

"These are my khala's daughters from Lahore, Laila and Zulekha. Twins, you know."

I just gaped at them. They were both extremely fair, pink and white really, and had green eyes and golden hair. Laila looked like a Moghul princess with a thick braid swinging to her hips, while Zulekha had a boy cut framing a very European-looking face. They didn't even look like sisters let alone twins, but they were both absolutely stunning.

"I know," Ghazala sighed.

"Yup." I could manage no more. The twins burst out laughing and in that instant we became friends.

The next day after lunch the four of us were in our room, ostensibly getting our clothes ready for the evening, when the topic of marriage was brought up by Ghazala.

"So is there any development on the Mansur front, Laila?" she asked.

Laila looked warily at *ayaji*, the maidservant whom her mother had brought along from Lahore and who was waiting to be told what outfits to iron for the evening.

"Oh, don't worry about *ayaji*," said Zulekha. "She is on our side. She will never tell on us, will you, *ayaji*?"

"No, no *beta*. You are my children. I am here to do your bidding."

"*Ayaji* sit down. Rest, it is siesta time. And this room is cozy and comfortable," Zulekha said.

"Well, I will straighten my back a little while you get your clothes out, but not for long. There is a lot to do." And *ayaji* stretched out on the carpet.

"So, Laila, tell us what is happening?" Ghazala asked again.

It turned out that Laila was in love with a young man who was with her at the National College of Art. He was eligible enough but there had always been a tacit understanding with one of her mother's friends that Laila would marry the friend's son. Now Laila was in a quandary about what to do.

"I don't know about this love business," Ghazala said. "One of my mother's friends had a love marriage and it turned out he was an alcoholic. She had to get a divorce."

"Our neighbor's daughter got married to someone that her family disapproved of," I added. "Her father didn't even attend the wedding. Only her mother was there. But that also ended in a divorce."

"Any marriage can be bad," Zulekha said, defending her sister. "Love marriages are not the only ones that end in a divorce. And Mansur is fine in every way. If Ammi had not made this arrangement with Saeeda Auntie, there would be no problem."

"I don't even know when and why this arrangement was made," Laila said, propping her head in her hand. "I was never asked. I feel so powerless. Zulekha, do you remember the time when our *dhoban* was about to get her son married to her niece? And he kept saying no but no one listened to him and how badly that ended? I feel like that poor fellow and dread the outcome. Oh, what am I to do?"

"What is this *dhoban* story? Out with it," Ghazala ordered, quite intrigued

Zulekha sat next to Laila on the bed. She kept one arm round her and with her other hand she gently brushed back golden tendrils of hair from Laila's face. After a short silence she told us the story.

The *dhoban's* son did not want to marry his cousin. But the *dhoban* insisted that the marriage had to take place since she had promised her brother that his daughter would marry her son. The battle of mother and son became epic. All the relatives found out and started taking sides. All the *dhoban's* clients told her not to antagonize her son by opposing his wishes in this matter. But the marriage took place despite their advice. The *dhoban's* son never went near his bride. Instead he signed up as a sailor in a merchant navy ship and left the country. The bride returned to her father's house and the *dhoban* was left hoping against hope for the return of her son. Unhappiness for everyone!

That story threw a pall over our spirits for a while. But soon Laila revived under Zulekha's ministrations and gave us the details of her first meeting with Mansur and how the relationship ripened into love. Yet, as I listened to Laila's love story all I could be completely convinced of was that she adored Mansur; about his feelings I was less sure.

I remained silent as the others deliberated ways of breaking the news to her mother. Many suggestions were made and discarded. Zulekha's idea was to be brutally honest and to just tell their mother about Mansur. Laila quailed at the thought. Ghazala recommended writing a letter to the parents in which Laila could bare her heart.

I could not keep my thoughts to myself any longer.

"Without a proposal of marriage from Mansur there is nothing for your parents to consider and nothing for you to tell them." I interrupted. "You have to convince your parents that both of you love each other. Unless Mansur demonstrates that he truly wants this union by proposing marriage his good faith will remain in doubt."

"But he doesn't want to be rejected," Laila wailed. "He can't propose knowing the answer will be no."

"Nothing ventured, nothing gained. If he wants to marry you he should show some guts. Why should you do everything?"

This caused both the twins to rally to Mansur's defense and enumerate all his good qualities. I did not contest Mansur's alleged virtues but did not back down from my stance either. A marriage proposal from him was essential. Without that I was not convinced about his love for Laila. He could just be enjoying a flirtation with the most beautiful girl in class.

Even as I reiterated my opinion I had a strange sense of déjà vu. I could hear my mother in my own words. Had I been so totally brainwashed that now I thought like her and spoke her words? What was I? A goody two shoes who was always obedient and docile? Ugh, no! Then why was I arguing against love?

In the middle of this argument *ayaji* woke up and asked again for the clothes that were to be ironed. I decided to solicit her support.

"*Ayaji,* what do you think? Should girls get married to people they fall in love with or to the person their parents choose for them?" I had worded my question in such a way that I was sure she would opt for the latter. But I was in for a surprise.

"*Beta*, marriage is a gamble. No one knows which one will work. It is all *kismet*. So I don't know what is best. But I pray that all girls have happy marriages."

She had a point. The stories related to me in the past months were full of misery in marriage and they were not all love marriages.

"*Ayaji*, you must have seen so much in your life," I said. "You tell us how to make sure a marriage works out."

Ayaji sat up and made herself comfortable as she leaned against the wall.

"*Beta* what can I tell you? I am illiterate. But I know you cannot escape your fate. I will tell you my own story and that will make you understand that humans are helpless at the hands of their destiny."

Then addressing Laila and Zulekha, *ayaji* told the following story.

THE STORY OF THE GULLIBLE BRIDE

I came to work for your aunt when Rafaat Bibi was born. I was the *ayah* and even though I had to leave my own children with my mother, I was glad to get the job. My husband had died of TB some months before and we had no money and no food. He was an educated man and worked in a newspaper office. But once he became too ill to go to office, his income stopped and we spent what little we had on his treatment.

First we took him to the doctor in our own *mohalla,* and he gave him injections every day. Each one cost Rs. 200. When that failed we went to a doctor in Saddar who was recommended by many of our relatives. Here my husband became even worse though we were giving him capsules costing Rs.75 each, which the doctor had prescribed. Finally when my husband started bringing up blood and all our money had disappeared, we took him to Jinnah Hospital. They said he had TB but that it was too late for him. We should have brought him in earlier.

But, *beta*, you know what it is like in Jinnah. It is free but thousands of people wait to see the doctors and sometimes your turn never comes and the day is gone. How could I have taken my ill husband there? What would people have said? Private doctors are supposed to be better. But we found that private doctors had been cheating us. At the end my husband was sent to Ojha Sanatorium but nothing could be done; the wretched disease had made a home inside my husband. It was his fate. He died and we began to starve.

The people of the *mohalla* tried to help. Many sent us food. But they were poor people. How long could they aid us? So I was happy to get a job with your aunt.

I began to love Rafaat Bibi almost as soon as I saw her. She was such a good baby, and I was missing my own children so I took her to my heart. On my weekly day off I would miss Rafaat Bibi even though I was surrounded by my own brood. When her younger brothers were born I became their *ayah* too but Rafaat Bibi had a special place in my heart always.

Then the children started school and my duties changed. I kept their rooms and their clothes neat and tidy and went with the driver to drop and pick them up from school every day.

My own children also grew up. Your aunt paid for their schooling. After Matric, your uncle helped the older one to enlist in the Navy and the younger one was sent to a good school to become an electrician. And when the time came for my daughter to get married your whole family helped me with the expense and your mother and aunt even came to the wedding. You have all been very good to me.

Your aunt often told me that because of my presence she had no worries about the house. She knew I would never take anything that was not mine and neither would I let any other servant do so. That house became my home since I had lived there longer than anywhere else. When your aunt told me that I would accompany Rafaat Bibi to her new house at the time of her marriage, I was content.

The rest of the servants were not my friends. They said I was madam's spy. I did not mind. My loyalty was always to your aunt and her family.

Then when Rafaat Bibi was in college a new driver was hired. Drivers came and went a lot in your aunt's house even though she was never bad to them. I think that is the way with drivers. They do not stay more than a couple of years at any one place. Anyway, the new driver, Kadir, was hired and things began to change in the kitchen.

Kadir was young and unmarried. He was always laughing and cracking jokes. Whenever he was in the kitchen between duties he would ask the cook for a cup of tea. At first the cook told him the rule of the house was tea twice a day for the servants. But Kadir wheedled and flattered him and finally the cook made him a cup, looking at me warily because he knew I would report it to your aunt.

But I never did so. Because of Kadir I was being included in every conversation in the kitchen. It made me feel good. So I kept quiet and soon it became a routine that everyone got tea at least two extra times a day.

Then Kadir started talking to me when we went to drop and pick up Rafaat Bibi. He would begin the conversation as soon as we were alone in the car. I had never let any driver take such liberties with me in the past. But Kadir had such an easy, friendly manner that I could not snub him. I started looking forward to our private chats in the car.

We talked about simple things. I told Kadir about my life. How both my sons were earning well and how I was saving my salary for my old age. They were good boys but they could change after they got married. A bit of money in hand oils the wheels of a family, so saving was important to me. Kadir told me about his life. His mother had died and his father had married again. There was no place for him in the new family so he left his village and came to Karachi. Now that he was a driver he was earning well for the first time.

One day Kadir got me a dozen blue glass bangles. I was so touched that I blushed. No one had given me a gift in my entire life. Then another day I was wearing one of your aunt's old *joras*, a pink one, and Kadir told me I looked good in those clothes.

What can I say *beta*? Now it all looks silly. But after a lifetime of drudgery those drives with Kadir made me feel good and slowly, slowly my heart mellowed toward him. When about a year later he asked me to marry him I agreed at once. Rafaat Bibi's wedding was arranged and she was to marry after only a few months. Your aunt was busy with all the preparations. It was understood that I would go with Rafaat Bibi to her in-laws and here I was planning my own marriage!

When I told my sons about Kadir they were very angry. They said they would not be able to look people in the eye if I got married at my age... and to a man younger than me. Kadir had told me they would say all this, so I was ready. I pointed out to my sons that when they got married their wives would be happy not to have a mother-in-law in the house. They still did not agree. Finally about two weeks before Rafaat Bibi's wedding Kadir decreed that we had to run away together without telling anyone. I thought I would lose him if I didn't agree. Even your aunt's salt, that I had eaten for years, did not stop me. On my day off Kadir came to my house and we went with a friend of Kadir's and got married in a mosque.

Oh! *Beta*! My eyes had been shut to reality till then. I had not even thought about where we would live and what we would eat. I only realized after the marriage ceremony that my job at your aunt's could not continue and that neither could his. So we ended up in the dark, cramped room in which his friend lived. It was damp and smelly and had no furniture except a string bed. By Allah's mercy the friend went away for two months to his village so we did not have to share the space with him. And, as you may know, we never had to plan beyond those two months in any case.

On the third day Kadir asked me for money. He said he wanted to start a business with a friend who was a car mechanic. The bastard told me that to become a partner he needed Rs. 30,000... the exact amount that I had told him I had saved. *Beta* I did not want to give him the money but he calmly opened my trunk and took it all. Once the money was in his hands I hardly saw him. He would return to the room late at night to sleep and if I asked a question he would give me one in the face.

Once or twice he did give me money for food. That was when he told me to cook a meal for his friends. I had to sit inside the hot room while they ate outside. I saved a few rupees each time for my own food but I became thin and ill and so ashamed. Then came a day when I threw up and knew I was pregnant. When I told Kader he beat me black and blue and kicked me out of the door.

I could not face my sons, but where else could I go? They were so angry, but they were good boys and they took me back. I could not return to your aunt; I could not face her. But I needed another job and that is when Allah led me to Shahnaz Begum.

With Shahnaz Begum I found a place to hide myself and my shame. I was so old, a grandmother, and now I was expecting a baby!

Shahnaz Begum treated me as if nothing was wrong. She did want to know the story but once I told her everything she never talked about it again. I looked after her two-year-old daughter and did the cooking while she was away at work. I never went home even for a day and never met my family. When the time came, Shahnaz Begum took care of the hospital bill and stayed home from work so that I could rest for a week. The first time my sons saw my baby she was one year old.

Shahnaz Begum must seem to you to be an angel to take such good care of me. And she was. *Beta*, no one does all that for a servant—even less for a new, unknown servant. You will understand her only if I tell you her story.

She was a beautiful lady from a rich family and she got married to a gentleman who had studied in England. He earned a great deal and they were rich and happy. Then he got cancer and nothing could be done for him. He was going to die. They had a daughter who had got married just that year and a son who was also studying in England. Before he died, the sainted gentleman gave his son the money he needed for his studies and then put the rest of the money in Shahnaz Begum's name. She was going to become a widow but she would be rich and need no one's help!

That is exactly what happened but you cannot escape *kismet*. Just like Kader, an evil man with a smile and a smooth tongue tricked Shahnaz Begum into marrying him. Since she was rich it took him a year and a half to clean her out completely. Then he disappeared and she was left with a daughter, just like me. When she heard my story she decided to help me. She was not rich anymore. After her second husband ran away she had to get a job for the first time in her life. She told me she got a good job because she was educated. But she had to work hard and forget all the luxuries of the past. Out of her hard earned money she helped me and my baby. She was so good; I pray for her every day. Allah made her heart soft for me. Otherwise who hires a pregnant maid or one with a small baby?

So, *beta*, neither money nor education can help you if unhappiness is written for you. I thought I fell for the scoundrel because I was illiterate. But Shahnaz Begum was educated and she had seen the world yet she was tricked too. I just pray that all girls have good marriages.

———— ((◦)) ————

With a sigh *ayaji* got up from the floor, collected our clothes and walked away to the ironing room.

"Wow! That was some story!" said Ghazala. "And I wonder who this Shahnaz Begum was?"

"This is nothing," I said. "I have been the recipient of endless tales of marital woe. Sometimes I feel marriage is actually perilous. But *ayaji's* story clearly shows that being impulsive when making such momentous decisions is not a sane choice. Marriage is forever and, girls, we should be happy to get as much help as possible in this matter."

"Stop with your lectures, Amna," said Zulekha. "Just because you have never fallen in love you can't dismiss it out of hand. Laila really loves Mansur and she can't even think of marrying anyone else. Nor can Mansur."

"Well then, you go and tell Mansur to come to your house with his parents. I will believe everything once he does that. And if he is as eligible as you say, your parents might even agree to the proposal. Why wouldn't they, once they realize that Laila wants it too?"

Ghazala came to the rescue. "Okay, okay, enough now. We can't settle this issue here and now. Ammi has told us to make sure the tables are laid properly. So let's go."

The party turned out to be fabulous. Two hundred guests, all decked out in their finest, assembled in the lawns of Ghazala's house. Her grandmother came and sat in the center of a semi circle of her closest relatives who then told true but funny anecdotes about her. Ghazala's grandmother countered by relating some really embarrassing episodes involving them. It was hilarious. The grandmother was tall and paper thin because of her recent illness but her mind was as sharp as ever and she was wickedly funny. After that we had a sumptuous dinner and slices of a huge chocolate cake which had been made in the shape of a sitar, an instrument that Ghazala's grandmother used to play in her younger days. At departure every female guest was given a gift from the birthday lady who made sure to say goodbye and thank you to each guest personally. She stood straight, her smile never slipped, and her eyes continued to twinkle till the last guests, my parents and I, left the party.

I did not meet Laila and Zulekha again since they had come just for the weekend but I mulled over the Mansur question in my own mind. Why was I so unconvinced about his intentions? I had always attended all-girls institutions and had not the vaguest idea how young men and women interacted on a daily, informal basis. But Laila was beautiful and I could imagine that many a male would like to make up to her. In all the novels I read, men under the age of twenty rarely had marriage on their minds. But their hormones were raging and a good flirtation, or more, was just up their alley. On the other hand the girl in question became dewy eyed and really fell in love...a recipe for heartbreak.

The thought that I was spouting my mother's lines from my mouth was disconcerting. I loved and respected Ammi but she was always logical and matter-of-fact and never any fun. Honest examination made me realize that I was also logical and practical. I couldn't stand fuzzy thinking and soppy emotional outbursts even in the novels I read. But I did like fun. My cogitations set my mind at rest. Clear thinking was a good trait even if it mirrored my mother.

Some days later I asked Ghazala what was happening in Laila's life but she had no news. So we concluded that status quo was reigning in the Laila/Mansur saga. And soon I became too engrossed in developments in my own life to give distant Lahore much attention.

Another doctor came to see me, and wonder of wonders it turned out to be a positively fun experience. The doctor was good looking and outgoing and really easy to talk to. He asked me how I liked college and when I said, "Good," he wiggled his eyebrows at me and said, "Really?" And I burst out laughing.

"Well, mostly. Sometimes it can be a bit of a drag," I added with a smile.

"I look back on my college years quite fondly now," he said, smiling. "But when I was going through them I liked only the exciting bits. The daily grind was just a necessary evil."

"You are right. The four years should be divided into two years for studying and the other two for unadulterated fun."

"What a good idea," he said. "And the boring students should be made to leave before the fun years began. No party poopers needed."

I laughed with him and suddenly noticed people were looking at us. A bit embarrassed, I started serving tea to the doctor's parents and sister with my gaze lowered. The encounter with this doctor, a neurologist to be exact, ended on an even better note when next day I was informed by Ammi that his parents had sent a formal marriage proposal.

I had found in my eighteen years that good usually comes with bad not far behind, and that is just what happened. A few days later Saima Phoopi and Zahid Bhai came over with a big box of traditional sweets. Zahid Bhai had got a job in Manchester in his chosen field of cardiology as a first step toward attaining MRCP. My parents congratulated them both wholeheartedly. But he was going away for four years and Nadeem bhai was also away. Who was going to be my champion now?

For the moment I tucked away my misgivings and joined in the celebration. Abba was ecstatic since his favorite nephew was following in his footsteps. Ammi was already planning a farewell dinner for Zahid Bhai. Poor Saima Phoopi was sad and happy at the same time. She would miss her son every day yet the path he had chosen was the only way to independence and prosperity.

"You are going to be near Nadeem Bhai," I chirped. "That will be a big support to him."

"Yes, indeed. And it will be wonderful to have a friend and cousin there when I arrive."

Ammi asked them to stay for dinner and we all talked till quite late about England and advanced degrees and future prospects. It was a happy evening. I told him of the neurologist.

"Do you know him, Zahid Bhai?"

"No, I don't think so. But I see you have taken quite a shine to him."

"Nah! But he was an improvement over the oddballs I usually encounter." I then turned to face him and said, "I will miss you tremendously, you know. You are the first friend I ever made."

"I will miss you too," he said. "Write often and tell me what is happening. I want to be a part of your life, always."

I could do no more than smile at Zahid Bhai mistily through my tears, nod, and pray silently that he would be a better correspondent than Nadeem Bhai.

CHAPTER 14

That day began like any other and I had no premonition that it would descend into the pits by evening. I returned from college and was told by Ammi to get ready by 6:30 since some people were coming to 'see' me. One of Abba's cronies, Imtiaz Uncle, had set up the meeting. The interested party was a major in the army and the son of an old pal of Imtiaz Uncle.

I changed into the Ammi approved clothes and did my hair. This had become so much of a routine that apart from a sliver of curiosity about the major I was quite relaxed. At the right time I pushed the tea trolley into the drawing room and went to sit at my designated seat. Even as I crossed the room I could feel the tension in the air. Ammi's back was rigid and her face set. Abba was visibly squirming in his chair and Imtiaz Uncle was studiously examining his shoes. I sat down just as the major spoke to the lady I took to be his mother. The other two guests were male, presumably his father and brother.

"No, no, Ammi, I became friends with Fatime after Ayse. Don't you remember Ayse had become so clingy? She had to be dropped."

"So difficult to remember all your girlfriends!" his mother tittered with pride. "When Faisal was in Turkey all the girls were after him, you know. He is so good looking. Girls just pursue him. It has always been this way."

I looked at the guest family as I listened. The father was short and thin with a receding hairline. The brother was younger than the major and had narrow shoulders and a chin innocent of hair. But his shirt buttons were open nearly to his navel and his cuffs were waving in the air, unbuttoned.

The major himself was tall and straight with a truly magnificent moustache. He could have played the villainous third party in a love triangle to perfection. But the most interesting was his mother. She looked older than Ammi but was dressed in a style favored by young teenagers. She was slim enough to carry the clothes but looked grotesque in the get up. She flung her head back coquettishly when she spoke and ended her sentences in girlish giggles. Her three men looked on with complacent pride.

"Mrs. Kamal, let me tell you that there is no lack of beautiful and rich girls for our Faisal," she continued. And I swear he sat up straighter and squared his shoulders with a self-satisfied smile. "But Bhai Imtiaz praised your daughter so much and kept on insisting we come to see her. Well, I finally agreed." She ended with a shrug and her *dupatta* slipped off her shoulders. Unfazed by the cleavage which was now staring us all in the face she went on. "Faisal loves me so much. My every wish is his command. So I said we have to go with Imtiaz Uncle today and he agreed."

In silence Ammi signaled me to serve the goodies from the trolley. In silence I got up to do her bidding, glad that I was not required to make small talk with this specimen.

"Both my boys pamper me all the time," the mother simpered. "They never want me to do any chores in the house. When I had flu last month you should have seen how they took care of me. Faisal cancelled all his dates. The telephone would not stop ringing as girl after girl begged him to go out with her. But he just said, "No, my mother is not well. I cannot leave her. She is more important to me than any of you."

I started feeling embarrassed for the two sons but, glory be, they were both smiling as if they had received a trophy at the hands of the president! This was certainly the strangest family to have crossed our threshold to date. As soon as I had passed the food to the guests I left the room without checking with Ammi. But I lingered by the door to see how Ammi was going to handle the situation. I need not have worried. She only allowed the guests to finish the food on their plates.

"Imtiaz Bhai, I am so sorry, but Kamal and I have to be at an official dinner tonight," Ammi said and then turned to the other guests. "I am sure you will understand and excuse us. These official things start so early." She stood up and so did Abba. Poor Imtiaz Uncle mumbled something in broken sentences and before the major and his family quite grasped what was happening they had been ushered out the door. What tactics! What strategy!

Once the three of us were alone I did not attack the trolley. I was so angry that I was close to tears.

"Ammi, must I be exhibited to such buffoons. I thought you were filtering out the undesirables. Don't tell me you thought this lot was acceptable."

Abba came and hugged me. "I am sorry, *beta*. It was my fault. Imtiaz talked me into letting these idiots come. Your mother was dubious about the whole affair." I burst into tears and had a good cry as Abba kissed and consoled me.

"Yes, this was a very bad experience, Amna. Your father has apologized. Now please stop crying. Go and wash your face and eat something."

I did as I was told but that night I couldn't sleep. I knew all Ammi's arguments yet I resented this repeated and relentless examination by strangers that I had to endure. It was demeaning in the extreme. I could not believe that all the girls of my age who were unattached were going through the same agony. I was certain my ordeal was longer and more intense because of my mother's drive for perfection.

Ghazala was so lucky. She got engaged to Sardar without meeting a single oddball. Ainee Auntie was a marvel. She did not subject Ghazala, even once, to being sized up and assessed by boors. A little worm of envy twisted in my heart. Ghazala had such an easy life. Her mother indulged her every desire. She had dozens of servants to do her bidding. In fact her house revolved round her and her needs. And she never had to get dressed and trundle the tea trolley for strangers. I had to remind myself that she had no father and that my father was the best Abba in the world. That soothed my bruised ego slightly and I fell asleep.

The next day at college I saw Ghazala coming toward me and immediately felt a renewed pang of jealousy. She had no idea what I had gone through the day before. She must have been relaxing all evening without a care in the world! But as she approached I saw something was wrong. This was not the normal bubbly Ghazala. In fact, her eyes were swollen and red. She either had a killer headache or she had been crying.

"What's the matter, Ghazala? Are you all right?" My simple inquiry caused her to fling herself into my arms and burst into tears.

"What has happened, please tell me. Is Ainee Auntie well?" I said with great concern.

It was some minutes before she could control her sobs and let the story tumble out of her. Ainee Auntie was fine. It was Sardar that she was worried about. For two whole months he had not written to her, even though she had been writing nearly every day. Even her anguished inquiries as to the cause of his silence had not wrung a letter from him.

"I think he doesn't like me anymore." She wept. "Perhaps he has found someone else there. Perhaps he has fallen in love!"

I had no idea why Sardar was not writing but I knew that there were better and easier ways of breaking an engagement. He could have just told his parents that he wanted an end to the relationship. He did not have to be so cruel. The Sardar I had met would not be so heartless.

"I think the letters have just gone astray," I said in a matter-of-fact way. "You are making a big deal out of nothing. What does Ainee Auntie think?"

"I haven't told Ammi anything yet. Amna, all the letters can't get lost. Something serious has happened."

"Well, if you think so we must make a telephone call to him. You have to tell your mother and speak to him directly."

We then walked quickly to the bathroom so that she could wash her face and fix her hair. I had to babysit her through each class, otherwise she would have broken down again. It was Shahida's birthday and we were all going with her for lunch at our favorite Chinese restaurant. We walked out at 12:30 in a group of seven. The best quality of the restaurant was that it was an easy walking distance from the college. During the lunch Ghazala was a little diverted and we all had a good time.

I called Ghazala later in the day to get an update. But Ainee Auntie had still not returned from her sister's house. Her niece's wedding was coming up and she was helping her sister in the last minute arrangements. Ghazala was crying again. I did my best to calm her and hung up after making her promise to call me the minute she had apprised Ainee Auntie of the situation.

It was after 8:00 p.m. when she called me back. Ainee Auntie had been told and she had immediately called Sardar but he was out. A message had been left for him. The waiting was causing Ghazala to get morbid again.

"I know, he will break the engagement and then no one will want to marry me. At least when people come to see you they like you. You are so pretty. But I will just get rejected and rejected and rejected." Ghazala ended in a hiccup.

"No, you won't," I countered, stoutly loyal. "And in any case Sardar will not do anything of the kind. He is not a cad. He is a good decent guy. It is just some logistical problem, nothing else."

"He is nice, isn't he?" Ghazala was momentarily appeased. "But then why doesn't he write?" She burst into tears again.

It turned out to be a pretty long call. When I hung up Ammi wanted to know what was happening. I told her the story for she was good in crises.

"There is nothing to worry about," she said calmly. "Sardar must be busy with work and has either not written yet or written a letter or two and forgotten to post it. Calling him is the best way to clear the air."

My gosh! I was becoming more and more like her. That is almost exactly what I had told Ghazala.

At 11:00 that night I got a call from a relieved and effusive Ghazala. All was well. Sardar had been busy and had written to her though only a few times. But he had left the letters near the bag which held the outgoing mail and not put them in the post box himself. He feared they had gotten lost. He was about to call her himself since her letters told him that she was not getting any mail from him. So all was well again with Ghazala and her dire predictions were forgotten.

On the other hand Ammi told me that Jamal Chacha's wife was bringing a cousin of hers the next day to meet me. So my sorry saga was to continue!

The next day at college Ghazala and I celebrated the normalization of her engaged status by going to the Chinese place again. Ghazala repeated her conversation with Sardar again and again and her face glowed with delight. With a resurgence that appalled me, my jealousy reared its ugly head. Why did she have to be exempt from being examined like a piece of raw meat? Why did I have to be the victim of this horrible tradition? With difficulty I hid my feelings from my best friend. Or perhaps she was too engrossed in her own happiness to notice my monosyllabic replies.

Clad in one of the approved *joras*, and with a sense of helplessness, I entered the drawing room behind the tea trolley once again that evening. The guy this time was a banker working for a foreign bank in Karachi. He was personable enough and had the social grace to initiate a conversation with me. I gave all the correct replies as I looked around the room. Jamal Chacha's wife was there, of course, and the banker's parents. They looked to be normal and middle aged, nothing to dislike there. I served tea to them and the mother engaged me in a brief conversation. All went according to schedule and the guests left about forty-five minutes after their arrival. Ammi urged Shama Chachi to join us in the tradition of eating heartily post guests, and I went to my room to finish a paper that was due soon.

On Saturday, Shama Chachi called. The banker's family had rejected me because, according to the mother of the banker, my mouth was too large. Too large? Was there a regulation mouth size that I had violated? I felt insulted and also blazingly angry. It wasn't as if they were the most beautiful people in the world themselves. How trivial-minded could you get?

My mother echoed my thoughts. "Well, we are well rid of such mean-spirited people. They looked acceptable but that just shows that looks can deceive. By the way, Amna, I hadn't told you yet but the major's family approved of you. I declined that proposal at once, as you can imagine." Ammi smiled.

Even though I held nothing but contempt for the major and his mother, their approval helped me to forget my large mouth.

Later the same week Ammi and Abba gave me a rundown of the six marriage proposals they had short listed. They included Saif, the architect, who was Shafiq Khalu's relative, the dark skinned engineer related to Hassan Khalu, the doctor who was Zahid bhai's friend, the unprepossessing BCCI guy and the neurologist.

"We are still making enquiries about each one," Ammi said, "but we thought we should ask your opinion about them too. Do you like or dislike any of them for any reason? Please don't hold back, this is a matter of your future."

I was silent. The BCCI guy was really plain and the engineer seemed unusually dark-skinned but did physical attributes matter? By dismissing those two I could be rejecting men who would make excellent husbands. If Ammi and Abba had shortlisted these six it meant they had found them, up to now, to be eligible in every way. My jabbing a spoke into the wheel could upset the entire process.

"No, I have no preference, Ammi. You and Abba decide and let me know," I said.

After a pause Abba spoke up. "Well, we will continue checking these six and then we will shorten the list to three and come back to you. Meanwhile if you need to tell us anything about any one of them, don't hesitate." And he gave me a hug.

I retreated to my room a little worried. Had I done the right thing by keeping quiet about the two whose appearance fell short of my expectations? Now that getting settled was coming closer and closer I was feeling quite scared. What was in store for me, or should I say who?

"Phone for you," Ammi called out as I wrestled with my thoughts.

I hurried to the phone in the lounge. It was Ghazala with news about Laila. Mansur had finally confessed that he could not ask his parents to formally propose for Laila's hand because he was already engaged to a cousin. Predictably, Laila was totally devastated. She had stopped going to college and was planning to drop out of NCA. Zulekha was doing her best to mend matters. Her parents were under the impression that Laila was finding college too difficult and had therefore fallen ill.

I thought of telling Ghazala to insist in her letter to Zulekha that the parents should be told of the situation. Zulekha could not protect and support Laila by herself. But did I really know enough to counsel others in this matter when I was so ambivalent about how much to confide in my own parents?

It wasn't easy to be eighteen, now nearly nineteen.

CHAPTER 15

That night I didn't sleep well. I had told my parents that I would abide by their decision for my future. What else could I have said? I knew no young men. I had never spent even five minutes alone with a young male who was not closely connected to me. What hope did I have to make the correct choice when it came to a husband? Actually the entire species of young males was foreign to me. I was so sheltered from reality that I had derived most of my notions of how the world worked from the novels I read. My life, though easy and comfortable, had not equipped me with the clarity of vision needed for selecting a life partner.

But if I was as unaware of the world around me as a newborn kitten with its eyes shut tight, should I be getting settled just yet? Ammi and Abba would do the best for me, I was sure. But what they deemed right for me now might turn out to be wrong as I matured. I did not want to get bound for life to someone whom I grew to hate just because I had agreed with my parents when I knew no better.

Ammi was going to be no help. She was sure to drag in the 'window of opportunity' business again. My only hope was to collar Abba and lay my concerns before him. Ammi and I were invited to Ainee Auntie's sister the next afternoon. All I had to do was to get out of the engagement somehow and waylay Abba when he returned from his clinic.

"I have a Sociology paper due tomorrow and I need to spend time in the library, Ammi. I might be a little late," I said the next morning at breakfast.

"Don't be too late. You know we have to go to Shireen's. I will iron your rose red jora. It is a wedding-related party and you must be dressed accordingly."

"Ammi, I am not sure I can go. It's a huge paper and will count toward our final grade. Besides, we will be going to three other functions of this wedding, so if I miss one it won't matter."

Ammi looked at me with narrowed eyes. "This must be some paper if you are willing to forgo being with Ghazala for a whole evening."

"No big deal. I will be with her the whole day!" I said and escaped.

That evening I remained in my room, at my desk, till Ammi poked her head in to tell me she was leaving. I smiled and waved, pulled out 'Sophie's Choice' and waited for Abba. As soon as I heard his car pulling into the driveway I flew to the front door.

"Hello, Abba."

"Hello, *beta*. I thought you had to go somewhere with your mother."

"I did but I had to study. Can I get you a cup of tea?"

He looked at me and paused. "That will be fine. Go and tell the cook to get tea for both of us."

On any other day I would have loved to sit with Abba and have a leisurely cup of tea. Under the circumstances, however, I just waited for him to finish his cup.

"Abba, I need to say something to you."

"Yes, I thought you might." His eyes twinkled.

"Abba, I don't want to get married or even get settled just yet," I blurted. Abba's amused look started to fade. I hurried on. "I know nothing of the world or about people. I don't even know much about myself. I will do whatever you and Ammi tell me to do but, Abba, what if you choose someone for me who would suit me now and then I grow and change and he is all wrong for the older me. I want to get married. But I want more than that. I want to study. I want a career. I don't want marriage to become my final destination." I ended breathlessly.

Abba pulled me close to him and started to pat my head gently. Finally he spoke," Your mother was your age when we got married and she took charge of us all. I know you could do the same, yet...."

I snuggled closer to Abba as I cudgeled my brain for other valid reasons to trot out for his scrutiny.

"But you are a baby still," Abba continued musingly. "There is plenty of time to get married. Marriage does not have to become your sole aim, specially now when things are in flux. Don't worry your head about anything. Ammi and I will talk things over. Now go and study." He kissed the top of my head as he got up and said, "I have some papers to read, *beta*, I will be in my room."

What had just happened? Did I win a victory or had I been brushed off with promises of candy like a four-year-old? Baffled, I returned to 'Sophie's Choice' and awaited developments. It was not a short wait.

The next two days went by in a strange state of limbo. Ammi and Abba directed only the most commonplace remarks at me, but I could hear the murmur of their voices behind the closed doors of their bedroom at the oddest hours. Was I the subject of their conversation? Or was it something totally unconnected?

Finally I was summoned to their room, which was strange since our family conclaves were generally held in the TV lounge. They were sitting side by side on the sofa. I plopped myself near Ammi's feet.

"Is everything all right?" I asked. They were both looking so serious.

"Yes. All is well. But we have to tell you something important," Ammi began. My heart pounded in my breast. Had they decided upon a mate for me? Or was I going to be allowed a reprieve of some years?

"*Beta*, I have been offered a job in Dubai," said Abba. "I have to give an answer in two weeks. Your mother and I have been discussing all the pros and cons of the change. We have also called Nadeem to get his input. Since you will be directly affected by the move, if we move, we'd like to talk to you about it too."

I was in a daze. I had heard nothing after Dubai. Unbelievable! I had not even figured in their nightly discussions. This was not about me at all. They were both looking at me expectantly. I was supposed to say something?

"Dubai?" I managed to squeak.

Ammi smoothed back my hair from my forehead. "Abba has been working very hard for a long time. If he takes this job he will get more money for shorter hours, much more money. We are financing Nadeem in England and that is an expensive business. If we stay in Karachi Abba cannot curtail his working hours and still provide for all of us."

"If we go to Dubai," Abba added, "We will be able to send you to a university in the UK."

"That's right," said Ammi. "We will rent out this house and that plus Abba's salary will be enough to cover the expense of sending you abroad."

I was stupefied. "You'll let me go to university abroad? Alone?"

"*Beta,* we are not blind. We know that you are bright. Dubai will allow us to open new doors for you." This came from Ammi! "You can do what your heart desires. We trust your instincts and we know you will make good choices."

"But I thought you wanted to get me settled."

"Yes, I did. But you and your father have convinced me that there is no hurry. And now there is this new option of moving to Dubai which means that you can go to the finest institution."

I leaned my head against Ammi's knees. "I thought you would not understand."

She smiled. I jumped up and hugged her and Abba. "Oh, thank you, thank you."

"Yes, that's all very well," Ammi continued, "but we have to weigh all the factors and then make this decision. Going to Dubai will mean leaving the family behind and saying goodbye to all your friends. We will all have to get used to new situations. And, worst of all, we will all be separated. The family unit will be dispersed."

"I don't know what my job will be like," Abba added. "Here I have made a name for myself. I have a reputation and I am well-known. There I will have to start from square one, so to speak."

"What we are saying is that there is a lot to think about before a final decision can be made. We want you to help us with this decision and we will keep talking to Nadeem as well. We have two weeks."

I returned to my room in a state of wonder. I had been offered far more than I had hoped for. Not in my wildest daydreams had I expected to study abroad. How could I when I was not even allowed to walk over to Azra Khala's alone, and she lived only two streets away from us? Yet my heart lurched at the thought of parting with everything that was familiar, even from Ammi and Abba. We would neither be a family, nor would we have a family home.

College could not hold my attention the next day. I told Ghazala everything at the first opportunity and both of us marveled at this turn of events.

"I can't even imagine you studying in an English university, far away from everyone."

"I know. Ammi was so cool about it as if it was no big deal; as if my life had not been hemmed in with ten thousand restrictions up till now!"

"And then you will become a career woman, Amna. My gosh, I don't think I know a single career woman."

"Nonsense, Ghazala, most of our teachers are female and therefore career women. Our doctor is a woman. Azra Khala is a career woman. Having a career is not going to set me up as a freak."

"No, silly, but you know what I mean. Most women do not work; they get married and are wives. But you will. Wow, I can't get over it."

"Well, that is, if Abba goes to Dubai."

"And you'll become rich. Remember when Khadija came back from Dubai? After only a year she had a Gucci handbag and matching shoes?"

"Yeah, but I don't see Ammi indulging me that much even in Dubai. And I don't even want the shoes and clothes. But going to a university in England! Wow! That will be something!"

Then it struck us that going to England would mean parting from each other. I knew that long distances were not easy to bridge. Already I felt I was losing Nadeem Bhai. Ghazala and I would certainly drift apart if our lives diverged radically. I would also be far away from my parents and Azra Khala and all my relatives and friends. But Nadeem Bhai would be close, and I would be doing what I had never dared imagine for myself. And the settling business would be postponed. I was selfish enough to be excited even though I could see Ghazala was close to tears.

The days of uncertainty continued. My brain became addled with so much serious thought. I was just a bit player in this drama and could only imagine the agonies my parents were going through. Upon their decision rested all our futures. We were fine as we were, but was Dubai going to be better? That was the question.

My birthday fell in the midst of all this indecision. No one had the heart to celebrate it with any fervor but something had to be done to mark my reaching the exalted age of nineteen. I invited Ghazala and Shahida for lunch at home and then we went to see the matinee show of the movie 'Alien.' Not on our own, of course. Ainee Auntie and Ammi also came but sat in a section far away from us. The two seats in front of Ghazala and Shahida were occupied by a young man and a *burka* clad figure whose face was covered by a *niqab*. We would not have given them a second thought but for what happened as soon as the lights were lowered. The lady flung open the *niqab* and was kissed by the young man with total abandon. The three of us could not tear our eyes away.

Ghazala leaned over and whispered, "I think this is what is called necking." I nodded speechlessly, and for the duration of the movie we found the antics of the two in front of us far more riveting than those of Sigourney Weaver. Was I glad that Ammi was not sitting by us! It would have been so embarrassing, a sort of trial by fire. At the end of the movie the *burka* clad lady, once again covered from head to toe, walked out with her companion. On the other hand the three of us were shaken and a bit subdued till Shahida said, "This is the only 'R' rated movie I have ever seen." That broke the spell and we were convulsed with laughter. It turned out to be a memorable birthday.

One evening in the following week Nafees Auntie came over. This time she had no one with her, but she came unannounced as always. Abba had not yet returned. I organized the tea and came in with the trolley. Ammi was telling Nafees Auntie about Dubai.

"Rabia, it is a wonderful opportunity. You must tell Kamal Bhai not to let it slip out of his grasp. I know of some other people, all professionals, who are going to Dubai. It is like winning the lottery, you know. They pay so well."

"Yes, that is so, but we are so well settled here, *Mashallah*. There doesn't seem to be any reason to forsake one's home. The only thing is that Kamal's timings there will be much better."

"Well, you are certainly a lucky woman. First of all, you have the luxury of making a choice, and then both the options are good. You can't go wrong."

"You are right, Nafees, we are very fortunate to have this choice."

"Oh dear," Nafees Auntie sighed. "That reminds me of Zebunissa, she was somehow related to my cousin. Her story is so sad. She almost never had the chance to make a decision for herself."

My heart sank. I could feel the advent of another sorrowful tale looming just ahead.

Nafees Auntie continued, "I will tell you her story because I think we tend to take our good fortune for granted. When you hear about people like her you are doubly thankful to Allah."

THE STORY OF THE FORGOTTEN DAUGHTER

This is the story of a woman whose life was so circumscribed by family and fate that she only had one opportunity in her life to choose a path for herself.

Zebunissa was born in Delhi in a family which was rich enough to be called *nawab*. Her mother died when she was five and her two younger brothers, Altaf and Affan, were toddlers.

Her father, Sheikh Waheed, was the only child of his parents, much indulged and pampered. As soon as his wife, Zebunissa's mother, fell fatally ill he became enamored of a woman of dubious virtue whom he had met on one of his forays into the red light district. He married her within days of his wife's death but kept the whole secret from his parents. He was dependent on his father for his monthly allowance and was genuinely scared of his autocratic mother. It was his mother, Bunyadi Begum, who had inherited the wealth from her father, and even though she seemed to defer to her husband she was the real force in the family and held the purse strings firmly in her grasp.

The marriage could not be kept secret after the birth of a son within a year of Zebunissa's mother's death. Sheikh Waheed finally told his parents of the new addition to his family. They were left angry and aghast by the revelation, but since he had presented them with a fait accompli they could do nothing. They refused to meet the new wife or son and Sheikh Waheed was admonished to find accomodations for them far from the family *haveli*.

Time passed and the new wife settled in her small house on the outskirts of the city and added two more sons to Sheikh Waheed's brood. Sheikh Waheed remained faithful to this new wife whose earthiness enchanted him far more than the prim ways of his first wife ever had.

In the *haveli*, the boys were sent to the best schools that Delhi had to offer but Zebunissa was tutored at home. She had a teacher for Arabic and Urdu and another, an Anglo Indian woman, to teach her English. Bunyadi Begum also saw to it that Zebunissa became adept at all the arts of homemaking. By the age of fifteen it was deemed that her education was complete and matchmakers were told to look out for a desirable match.

Before much progress was made Sheikh Waheed's father died after a short illness. The *haveli* was plunged into mourning and thoughts of matchmaking were forgotten. After the forty days of strict mourning were over Sheikh Waheed confronted his mother and suggested that he look after the affairs of the estate as his father had done.

"Never," Bunyadi Begum said. "If you wanted that, you should not have married a woman who is unfit to clean out the latrines.

It is my property and I am quite capable of looking after it with my staff."

Sheikh Waheed left in a huff, secretly thankful that Bunyadi Begum had not threatened to cut off the monthly stipend.

The strife in the house had the inevitable consequence of dividing family loyalties. Zebunissa's brothers, whose lives outside the *haveli* were free and easy because of the liberal temperament of their father, sided with him. Zebunissa, who rarely met her father and whose entire life revolved round her home, became a partisan of her grandmother.

Since Bunyadi Begum and Sheikh Waheed lived in separate houses the atmosphere in the *haveli* did not change much, but the matter of Zebunissa's marriage became a bone of contention. Sheikh Waheed was adamant that he would consider marriage proposals only if he were allowed to manage the estates, and his mother could neither agree to that nor accept a proposal and proceed with Zebunissa's wedding without her father's consent. Zebunissa's contemporaries started getting married and having babies, but her father and grandmother were unable to settle their differences.

Then one day, like a clap of thunder, as it seemed to Bunyadi Begum, the country was on the point of being divided. Muslims were packing up and leaving for their new homeland. The manager of her estate came to talk to her about what should be done.

"Done!" she said. "Nothing is to be done. For four hundred years my ancestors have owned these lands and have lived here. Why would I want to leave and go to some unknown place?"

Sheikh Waheed was immersed in his pleasures and Pakistan was far from his thoughts. But Altaf and Affan were both fervent supporters of the new nation. They had been working as volunteers with the Muslim League and wanted to follow their leader, Jinnah, wherever he led. Bunyadi Begum told them not to be silly. This was their land and this was where they would stay.

All around the *haveli* the upheaval became more intense. At night, fires could be seen burning whole swaths of homes and gunfire could be heard day and night. Food stuffs disappeared from the markets. Shortly no servant was willing to leave the *haveli* in search of staples. Then defections began. The servants left with their families to escape the mayhem in the city.

Finally the day came when the manager said he could not continue to serve his mistress of forty years. He was leaving with his wife and children for the safety of Purana Qila and thence to Pakistan. Bunyadi Begum called for her son now that the conditions were critical. Muslims were not safe anywhere. The government was urging them to leave their homes, as it could not guarantee their safety in their *mohallas*. Droves of Muslims were either fleeing the city altogether or seeking shelter in Purana Qila as they waited for transport to Pakistan.

Bunyadi Begum and Sheikh Waheed were completely out of their depth. Their past experiences helped them not a whit in the face of imminent danger and puzzling uncertainty. They finally fell in with the wishes of Altaf and Affan. There did not seem to be any other viable option. They decided to leave as soon as possible. The two boys were sent to book seats in the trains taking refugees to Lahore. Sheikh Waheed consoled Bunyadi Begum with promises of returning when conditions improved and selling off the property. Oh, for the bliss of ignorance: The son did not realize that he would never again return to the city of his ancestors, nor that selling her forefather's property was even more of a heartbreak for Bunyadi Begum than abandoning it.

Preparations for the departure started in earnest in the *haveli*. Sheikh Waheed went off to alert his other family. Bunyadi Begum supervised the sewing of money belts for each person. After money and jewelry were made snug in them, the belts would be tied around the bare waist and then covered by clothing. Each person would also have a capacious cloth satchel with important papers and sterling silver pieces wrapped in changes of clothes. Movable items were put into storerooms and locked. Furniture was covered with sheets. Meals were cooked for the journey and extra food was distributed among the *haveli* retainers who were leaving to make their own way to safety. Only Sher Ali, the old doorman, was left to sit outside the *haveli* door.

As the sun started to set, the two women in the *haveli* waited and worried. There was no word from Altaf and Affan who had been gone for hours. No servant was available to be sent out to look for them. Bunyadi Begum spread out the prayer mat and prayed for her grandsons. Every time a shot was heard it seemed to her to be aimed at Altaf and Affan and her prayers became more fervent. Zebunissa also tried to pray but her state of near collapse left her unable to articulate pleas to Allah. Then suddenly there was the sound of many running feet coming toward the *haveli*. Voices were raised in anger and there was a loud knocking on the door. Bunyadi Begum and Zebunissa cowered in fear, holding each other and moaning. The door was in danger of breaking under the assault. Should they hide? Should they open the door?

The spell was broken by a loud report of gunfire nearby and then what sounded like curses and fleeing footsteps. The door of the *haveli* opened and Altaf's voice was heard.

"Where is everyone? Why is it so dark?"

The two women ran toward him and his brother in relief and gathered the two boys in close embrace. A mob of Hindus had come to attack the *haveli*. Poor Sher Ali had nothing but his knife to save the honor of his masters. He fought, cut and bleeding, till Altaf and Affan returned. Altaf fired shots in the air and the mob scattered. There was easier prey elsewhere and many of their leaders had already been the victim of Sher Ali's knife thrusts. Once the mob retreated Altaf and Affan entered the *haveli*.

They were dirty and disheveled. It had been a momentous day. The railway station had been jammed with hysterical Muslims trying to flee the city. The police were powerless. They only got the tickets because they saw a school friend close to the ticket window. He bought tickets for them as well when his turn came. Coming back home was another hurdle. Bands of Hindus and Sikhs were roaming the street in search of Muslims to harass, loot or even kill. Altaf and Affan took detours, hid in doorways and, with great good luck, managed to reach their own home in safety.

At about this time Sheikh Waheed also returned, alone. He told the family that his wife would not be coming with them. Bunyadi Begum was glad not to be saddled with a low born daughter-in-law in the new land to which they were heading. Sheikh Waheed's wife had laughed in his face when he had urged her to pack for the journey. She said that women like her had no nationality and she would not leave her old support system to accompany a newly impoverished, middle-aged man. Neither would her children.

The family ate what they could and retired.

The next day dawned like any other but it would be a day that no one would ever forget. They were leaving behind all that they had ever known and ever possessed. With heavy hearts they tied their money belts to their waists. Bunyadi Begum had never gone out of the *haveli* except in a palanquin. Now she would be among strangers for the first time. She donned a black *burka* and gave a large *chadar* to Zebunissa to wrap herself in from head to toe. Their outer coverings hid their satchels to perfection.

Altaf and Affan were sent to get two *tongas* to transport the family to the station. Bunyadi Begum sat holding a healthy bunch of keys. For the first time in half a century they had become superfluous. She put them down by the water pot and headed toward the door as she heard Altaf's voice. In the first *tonga* sat the mother and son, and the three siblings climbed into the other. Just as the horses began to move, a screaming, *lathi*-bearing mob turned into their lane and rushed toward them. "*Chalo, chalo.* Go, go," screamed Altaf, but the mob started to hit the horses with their *lathis*. Altaf stood up and fired two shots in the air. There was dead silence for a moment. The mob hesitated. "*Chalo, chalo,*" Altaf screamed again and the horses sprang forward. But as the *tonga* streaked past the bloodthirsty crowd, someone pulled Altaf to the ground by his leg. The mob was upon him in a trice pummeling him with kicks and sticks. All Zebunissa could see was a pile of humanity upon the place where her brother had fallen; then the *tonga* turned the corner.

The family did get on their designated train and even reached Lahore the next day. They saw other refugees falling onto their knees to kiss the soil of Pakistan while they stood with staring, tear-less eyes. Their loss was too raw.

In a few weeks they were installed in a small house in the Old City. It had been vacated by a Hindu family fleeing east. But the whole tenor of the family had changed. Bunyadi Begum, the arch matriarch, had shrunken to a husk. The loss of her financial domi-nation had been trumped by the loss of a much beloved grand-son. She stayed in the room allotted to her and mumbled over her prayer beads when not prostrate on the prayer mat. She had no idea who was running the house, or doing the housework, neither did she care. Affan, left inconsolably alone, got admission to college and spent almost all waking hours away from the family. Sheikh Waheed soon located *Heera Mandi,* the red light district of Lahore, and felt quite at home in the new nation. Zebunissa had to take up the reins of the household perforce. She cooked, cleaned and tended to her grandmother singlehandedly. Affan would get her the groceries and other items needed in the house, but for the rest she was the mistress and the maid of this reduced establishment.

As Zebunissa braided her hair every morning she wondered what would happen to her. Now that her grandmother had retreat-ed from the world there was no one to worry about her marriage. Affan was too young, and too hurt, to think of nuptials and her fa-ther was, as ever, more concerned about himself.

In about a year's time Sheikh Waheed managed to spot some rental property within his means. He disposed of pieces of his mother's priceless jewelry to purchase it. The small but steady in-come was enough for him to be known, once again, as a *nawab* in the red light area. He was content.

One day Affan did suggest to his father that the time had come to think of Zebunissa's marriage. Sheikh Waheed silenced him by saying that he had lost touch with his friends from Delhi and the Punjabis wanted a dowry that he could not afford. Since Affan was himself dependent on his father's bounty he did not pursue the matter. Zebunissa, who had been listening to this exchange from the kitchen, began to pin her hopes on Affan's graduation and subsequent financial well- being. Then he would take care of his sister, she believed.

But it was not to be. Affan got a job with an oil company in Karachi after graduation. He escaped from his father's house with a sigh of relief and only returned three years later for his grandmother's funeral. During these years he had married his boss's daughter and decided to forget his lecherous father, his grief-stricken grandmother, and his down-trodden sister. He did not even invite his family to his wedding, explaining to his in-laws that his grandmother was too old and ill to travel or be left alone. It was a new beginning for him and he did not want it marred by the shadow of familial problems.

In the three years that Affan had been away in Karachi, Zebunissa had come to realize that he was going to do nothing for her. She feared she would die in the house in which she was effectively incarcerated since Sheikh Waheed, however licentious his own behavior might be, was too strict to allow his daughter to step outside the house alone. Her only company was her grandmother who almost never spoke and who needed to be taken care of like a baby. But even the solace of service to her grandmother ended when the old woman quietly passed away. Zebunissa cheered up when Affan came for the funeral. But he had come alone and left the next day.

Now Zebunissa's life took a turn for the worse. Her father installed Bulbul, a 23-year-old from *Heera Mandi* in the house, as his wife. Zebunissa was expected to continue doing the house work and even pander to her stepmother's whims. Sometimes when she was chopping vegetables, Zebunissa would look longingly at the knife in her hand and it was only her strong belief in the sin of suicide that kept her from using it on herself. She felt she was shriveling up inside. Even her vocal chords were atrophying for lack of use.

Automatically shutting out the sounds of giggles and grunts coming from her father's bedroom one morning, she smoothed out the newspaper in which coriander had been wrapped. She looked down and saw that it was a page of matrimonial ads. She pushed away the coriander stalks and bent down to read what other people wanted in their lives. Only young and educated brides seemed to be in demand.

Suddenly she stopped and bent down closer to read the ad which had caught her eye. "Government servant, 45, wants to wed pleasant-faced woman, 25 to 35, from good family." She had all the three attributes sought! She reread the ad to make sure. It was now or never, she realized. If she answered this advertisement, bad, bad things could happen but if she didn't she would just wither and fade away. As she struggled with her thoughts her hands tore out the ad and slipped it under the paper lining of the spice cabinet.

When her father and Bulbul went out for the evening she composed an answer to the ad and the next morning when the vegetable vendor came to the door she gave it to him to post. Now all she needed to do was to wait.

She did marry the government servant and bad things did happen. He turned out to be fifty years of age with one wife and one ex-wife. The first one was childless and had been relegated to a corner of the house when he married a second time. But his second wife came from a well-to-do and supportive family. When she discovered the existence of a first wife she returned to her parents' house and sued for divorce.

Sheikh Waheed had no reason to oppose the wedding. Bulbul disliked the constraints put on her by the presence in the house of a strait-laced and unmarried stepdaughter and the government servant, Nazim by name, made no demands for dowry. Affan loathed the aging roué on sight, but kept his own counsel. He did not want to disturb the precarious balance which allowed him to lead his life according to his own lights.

This was the only time that fate had given an opportunity to Zebunissa to decide for herself. She was determined to escape from her father's house even though she was not unaware that the route she was taking was fraught with dangerous uncertainties. In this case, the unknown seemed infinitely better than the familiar. Zebunissa grabbed at the chance of not happiness so much as a less miserable existence.

So the wedding took place with a minimum of fanfare and

Zebunissa went to live in his small house with Nazim and his first wife. The marriage was neither good nor bad. Zebunissa had low expectations from the union and she did not have to revise her estimate. Akhtari, the first wife, was verbally abusive during the day but docile when Nazim returned. Zebunissa managed the house with the money she was given every month. She garnered no companionship from her spouse, but then she was used to being alone since her grandmother's death. Happily, she became pregnant within months.

When Anis, the son, was about five and had just started regular school, Nazim was transferred to another city. Zebunissa flatly refused to leave with him. She saw no reason to dislodge herself from the place she knew. Nazim threatened to take Akhtari along instead. Zebunissa said that she would welcome that. In the event, Nazim left both the women behind and some months later the news filtered back that he had taken another wife. At the same time the small amount of money he sent every month to Zebunissa dried up.

Zebunissa began tutoring students in Urdu and held Quran classes for the *mohallah's* women and children. The meager amount she made this way was supplemented with occasional help from Affan. Akhtari continued to live with her since she had no place to go. As time passed the two women became friends and Anis often felt he had two mothers.

After Matric, Anis worked in a bank in the mornings and attended evening classes at a local college. Affan's help was not needed anymore. When Anis completed his Masters degree and got a prestigious job at a bank it seemed that Zebunissa's life had not been lived in vain. Affan sent the young man Rs. 5000 as a gift and both Akhtari and Zebunissa envisioned a future of ease and comfort.

That was not to be. Zebunissa was diagnosed with mouth cancer and died in great pain some months later. Akhtari nursed her like a sister. Neither Nazim nor Sheikh Waheed attended the funeral.

Did Zebunissa make the right choice the one time she had the chance? She thought so. As a consequence, she faced joy and despair, many ups and even more downs. But she was her own mistress and, to an extent, in control of her life.

⎯⎯➤«◉»⎯⎯

The story ended and there was silence as the minutes ticked by.

"Uff, Nafees, how terribly sad!" Ammi sighed. "You are right we have so much to be thankful for. Our lives have been singularly free of upheavals and adversity. And even now both our options are desirable. I just pray that we make the right decision for everyone so that the future is also happy."

"You will. *Inshallah*," Nafees Khala said with conviction." And now may I have some tea and a slice of your excellent banana nut cake. I should get the recipe before you leave."

She departed before Abba came in accompanied by Zahid Bhai who had been busy making arrangements for his own departure and had not visited us for some time. Now Ammi and Abba told him of the Dubai option and all the pros and cons were repeated for him. He listened without interrupting.

"Kamal Mamun, I think you want to go to Dubai," he said after a pause.

"Why do you say that?"

"Because you have made such a wonderful reputation for yourself here after years and years of selfless hard work, yet you are contemplating abandoning it all. It can only be because you are attracted to the Dubai idea."

"You are right, *beta*. Both the money and the working hours are better there. I have worked hard here, as you say, and have set my department at the hospital on the right path. I think it will continue to work well even without me. I want to slow down but not to retire." Abba laughed and went on. "I can't retire just yet, anyhow. Nadeem needs help and we are now thinking of sending Amna to England to study."

Zahid Bhai smiled at me. "Studying abroad? Then what about getting settled?"

"Well, that would have to be postponed for the time being," Ammi said.

Zahid Bhai gave me a knowing look and I smiled back.

"What? Why are you two smiling so mysteriously?" Ammi asked.

"It is nothing. Just that Amna had not wanted to get settled just yet and now her wish will come true."

Ammi was not pleased. "How many people have you been confiding in, Amna? I think you are old enough to know which topics can be discussed with others."

Before I could formulate an answer, Zahid Bhai sprang to my defense.

"Rabia Mumani, I just filled the place left vacant by Nadeem's absence. Obviously, Amna did not tell anybody else."

"Rabia, Amna can certainly talk to Zahid," said Abba. "He is a member of this family too. Anyway, it is water under the bridge. When are you planning to give us dinner?"

Over dinner the Dubai option was further thrashed out. It was much hotter there than Karachi and most people lived in apartments rather than houses. Strangely enough, Urdu was spoken widely so no one needed to learn Arabic.

I sat silently and daydreamed not of Dubai but of a verdant English university, full of quadrangles, where I would be engaged in lofty discourse with world renowned professors.

EPILOGUE

My castles in the air started to take concrete form the day that the Dubai job was officially accepted by my father. I didn't know whether to be happy or sad. There was no time to think. My exams were round the corner and I had to do well since the result would help in acquiring admission in the UK. Everything was in turmoil. Miles of red tape were required in clearing the way for Abba's early retirement. Visas to Dubai needed another mountain of paperwork. And Ammi was going through the house like a tornado throwing out everything she considered unnecessary so that the house was uncluttered for prospective tenants. Yes, we were renting out the dear house, completely furnished, and only taking our personal items, like clothes and books and pictures with us. Some of Nadeem Bhai's stuff was to be put in storage at Azra Khala's and all the rest was to be given away to charity.

I tried to focus on my studies but it wasn't easy. I had also to sort out all the information that Hassan Khalu had sent me about universities in Manchester. That was where I was headed so that Nusrat Khala could keep an eye on me. She was a sweetie pie so I didn't mind her chaperonage. Farida Khala would have been a fire-breathing dragon in the same position as would also Tahira Khala, especially after the Saif episode. Saif! I remembered that he too would be somewhere in the UK. Who knew, we could actually stumble upon one another someday; stranger things have happened. Even if Ammi and Abba were stuck in the desert, it was a consolation to know that Zahid Bhai would also be in Manchester and Nadeem Bhai close by in Liverpool.

I was going to study Clinical Psychology. It was touted to lead to a great many desirable careers. In reality I had chosen psychology because of my experiences during the past year. Ammi's desire to settle me had allowed me to meet such diverse people and hear such astonishing stories that it had awakened in me an interest in my fellow creatures. The range of motivations which instigate human behavior had become something I wanted to examine at length. Who knew where it would lead me?

The one thing that was certain was that change was in the air. My mother had changed. She was ready to overlook the 'window of opportunity' and even allow it to shut in my face. She may have made a deal with Abba by giving in to his will in this matter so that she could convince him to take the job in Dubai. She was really scared that Abba would work himself to death in Karachi as he toiled to provide for us all. Dubai was the ideal solution: more money but way less work. Abba was not enamored of Dubai, for going there meant getting somewhat sidelined. But he gave in to Ammi and won for me a life that would be radically different from the lives of women in his generation. He had seen what the lack of financial independence could do in the case of his own sister. He never talked of Saima Phoopi without adding the sobriquet 'poor' to her name.

There was change in that quarter too. Zahid Bhai was off to England and, if all went according to plan, we were to fly together to London when the time came. Then Nadeem Bhai would escort me to Nusrat Khala and my new life would begin. It was terrifying and exhilarating at the same time!

In all this upheaval there was also socializing. Nani and Lubna Khala were coming from Multan to say goodbye since we were too busy to visit them. Every evening Ammi and Abba were out to some farewell party or other. Ghazala was nearly a fixture at our house. She was prone to dissolving into tears at a minimum of once a day. Whenever there was a free moment in my study schedule Ammi dragged me out shopping. I needed a whole new wardrobe for Manchester.

I had no time to sleep or eat but I was happy. I was not getting settled! Instead, I was about to set out on the adventure of a lifetime. And what would happen regarding the six short-listed suitors? Ammi had called each one and told them I was going to university in the UK and that if after I finished they were still interested they could come and meet me again. But that was three years in the future and much could happen in three years!

My world was opening up and I was ready to embrace it.

The end

MRS. BHIMJEE'S RECIPES

Yakhni Pulao

For the Yakhni:
2 lbs or 1 kilo chicken with bones. Skinless and cut up
1 medium sized onion. Peeled, whole
4 cloves of garlic. Unpeeled, whole
2 inch piece of fresh ginger
8 black pepper corns
6 cloves
2 teaspoons white cumin seeds
5 cups* water

Boil everything together. Once it boils, lower the heat and let simmer till the meat is tender. Pour the whole through a sieve so that the soup (yakhni) is separated. Reserve. Save the chicken pieces also and discard everything else.

Pulao

2 cups basmati rice
2 tablespoons plain yoghurt, whipped
2 inch long cinnamon stick
2 teaspoons white cumin whole
4 cardamoms
3 bay leaves
1 medium sized onion sliced thinly
4 cloves of garlic peeled and sliced thinly

¾ cup cooking oil
2 teaspoons salt
Saved cooked chicken and yakhni

Wash rice and leave to soak in water.

Preheat oven at 200 C or 350 F

Choose a cooking pot which can cook 3 cups of rice easily.

In the pot heat the oil and saute onion till golden brown. Take the onion out on paper towel. Reserve. Add garlic to the oil and cook till it just changes color. Add cinnamon, cumin, cardamoms and bay leaves. Then add the cooked chicken and yoghurt and saute till the yoghurt disappears, about 2 minutes.

Add rice, being careful to keep out the water in which it was soaking. Stir gently and then add 3 and ¾ cups of yakhni. If there is not enough yakhni, add water to make up the measure. Add salt and bring to a rolling boil. Add the reserved fried onions and cover the pot with a tight lid. 2 layers of newspaper or aluminium foil can also be put between the lid and the pot to make it tight.

Place pot in preheated oven for 40-45 minutes. The pulao is ready when the rice has absorbed all the water and is cooked through. Serve hot.

Green Eggs Sandwiches

Filling:
2 hard boiled eggs. Peeled and mashed with a fork
2 tablespoons mayonnaise
1 tablespoon yoghurt
1 tablespoon finely chopped fresh coriander
1 tablespoon finely chopped fresh mint
Salt and freshly ground black pepper to taste
1 capsicum thinly sliced
Mix all together except for capsicum. If filling seems too dry add a little more yoghurt.

Sandwiches:
8 slices good brown bread, with the crusts removed
Spread filling on 4 slices of bread. Top with capsicum. Cover with the other 4 slices. Press down and cut into half crosswise. Makes 8 triangles.

*Cups meaning an 8 oz fluid measure

GLOSSARY OF URDU WORDS

Alu gosht: Meat and potato curry

Ameen: Literally Amen. A ceremony to celebrate the completion of Quran reading by a child

Apa: Older sister

Ayah: Nanny

Ayaji: Respectful way of addressing a nanny

Bakra Eid: Muslim holiday, the Feast of Sacrifice

Beta: Literally son. Used as a term of endearment for young people of both genders

Bhabi: Brother's wife

Bhai: Older brother

Bibi: Word servants use to address an unmarried daughter of the house

Biryani: Meat and rice dish

Burka: A full body loose covering, usually of black cloth, worn over clothes

Chacha: Father's brother

Chachi: Chacha's wife

Chadar: A large piece of cloth used to cover oneself

Chakri: A card game with 6 players

Chalo: Let's go

Chana chaat: Savoury dish made of boiled chickpeas

Chappati: Unleavened bread

Dargah: Mausoleum of a holy man

Data sahib: The mausoleum of the saint Data Ganj Bakhsh in Lahore

Dhoban: Laundress

Djinn: Genie

Dukh: Pain

Dulhan: Literally bride. Used to address the wife of a son or younger brother

Dupatta: Long scarf. Part of the three piece ensemble worn by Pakistani women

Eid: Muslim Holiday to celebrate the end of Ramzan

Fajr: One of 5 Muslim prayers, said before sunrise

Ghalib: Famous Urdu poet of the 19th century

Gham: Sorrow

Haleem: Meat and lentil dish

Harira: Thin wheat porridge made for invalids

Harrafa: Derogatory term to denote a conniving female

Haveli: Large mansion built in the style of 18th and 19th century Indian architecture

Inshallah: God willing

Isha: One of 5 Muslim prayers, said at night

Jama masjid: Main mosque of a city

Janoo: Term of endearment, like darling

Jora: Three piece ensemble which is the Pakistani national dress for women comprising of dupatta, qameez, shalwar

Khala: Mother's sister

Khalu: Khala's husband

Kheer: Pakistani rice pudding

Khuda hafiz: Good bye. Literally: May God protect you.

Kichri: A rice and lentil dish made for invalids

Kirpan: Short sword or knife with curved blade

Lathi: Stick

Mamun: Mother's brother

Mannat: A vow made to do something if one's wish is fulfilled

Mashallah: By the Grace of God.

Maulvi: Muslim religious scholar

Mohalla: Community

Motia: Small, white, fragrant flower, a little like jasmine

Mughlani: A female descendent of the Moghuls working as an upper class servant

Mumani: Mamun's wife

Naan: Leavened flat bread

Nawab: Landed gentry

Nikah: Legal marriage ceremony. The equivalent of the church or registry office ceremony

Niqab: Face veil

Pakola: Pakistani brand of soda

Pandan: Betel nut box

Parathas: Fried flat bread

Pathan: Native of Khyber Pakhtunkhwa, one of the provinces of Pakistan

Phoopi: Father's sister

Punjabi: Native of Punjab, one of the provinces of Pakistan

Qameez: Tunic, one part of the three-piece ensemble worn by Pakistani women

Qorma: Spiced meat curry

Ramzan: The Muslim month of fasting

Razai: Pakistani duvet

Rupee: Pakistani currency

Saafa: Turban

Sahib: Equivalent of Mr.

Samosa: Meat or potato-filled fried patty

Sehri: Meal eaten before sunrise after which Muslims fast till sunset

Shalwar: Baggy trousers, one part of the three-piece ensemble worn by Pakistani women. Also the traditional, baggy trousers worn by men

Shalwar qameez: Two words used to denote the national dress of

Pakistani women

Shamiana: Colorful Pakistani marquee

Sherwani: Pakistani national dress for men. A tight-fitting long jacket

Sindhi: Native of Sindh, a province of Pakistan

Sivayan: Vermicelli

Surma: Ultra fine black powder used as a cosmetic to make eyes prominent

Tola: Measure to weigh precious metals. About 10 grams

Tonga: A one-horse carriage used as a taxi before the advent of automobiles and, later, in rural settings

Valima: Dinner hosted the day after the wedding by the groom's family

Wadera: Feudal owner of large agricultural tracts in Sindh

Wuzu: Ablutions mandatory before offering Muslim prayers

Yakhni pulao: Meat and rice dish

Zuhr: One of 5 Muslim prayers, said around noon

ACKNOWLEDGEMENTS

The book would never have been written if my children, Murad and Nigar, had not insisted that I should write one. I began writing because I ran out of excuses.

My thanks go to my friend Amna Azfar, who generously offered to edit the book's first draft.

I am grateful to Mariam Qureshi who said, "A thousand times yes!" when I wondered whether she would design a cover for the book. Thank you, Mariam, for the perfect image.

I thank Lorna and, even more, Tom Pryor whose unstinting support made the book see the light of day. Thank you also for the painstaking proofreading which you both so willingly undertook.

Notwithstanding her myriad responsibilities Nigar, my daughter, spent hours assisting and encouraging me. She solved my tech problems, read the first draft and helped me with publishing decisions. Finally, she proofread the work for me.

Ali, my grandson, was brilliant at helping me compose the back cover text. Thank you, Ali.

The support of my husband, Rahat, was the most valuable. He has always believed, implicitly, that I can do anything. I thank Allah and my mother for arranging my marriage to him, all those years ago.

CPSIA information can be obtained
at www.ICGtesting.com
Printed in the USA
LVHW031503040619
620111LV00005B/873/P